The Ultimate Guide To Internet Marketing For Dentists

CHRIS PISTORIUS

www.ifusedentalmarketing.com

iFuse Dental Marketing serving Dentists nationwide. Proud members of the Catalyst Google+ Local Search Pro Team and a Google Certified Professional.

www.ifusedentalmarketing.com

Copyright © 2014 Chris Pistorius
All rights reserved.
ISBN: 150272040X
ISBN-13: 978-1502720405

www.ifusedentalmarketing.com

Contents

Introduction

Chapter 1	What Is Local Marketing?	(1)
Chapter 2	Why Local Marketing For Dentists?	(6)
Chapter 3	Dental Marketing Power Tools	(11)
Chapter 4	How To Do Dental Marketing The Right Way	(21)
Chapter 5	Highly Effective Marketing Tips	(67)
Chapter 6	Shocking Case Studies	(71)
Chapter 7	Dental Marketing Do's & Don'ts	(78)
Chapter 8	Video Marketing	(82)

Conclusion

www.ifusedentalmarketing.com

Introduction

When was the last time that you used a phonebook? When was the last time you actually picked up a telephone book and used it to find information on a local business? When was the last time that you picked up a local newspaper and proactively looked for display ads from local businesses? Do you often open up the mailbox with anticipation and hope that there will be tons of new postcards and letters from businesses trying to sell their services? Now, I am not saying that those advertising methods cannot be effective, but I am saying that by far it is not the most effective for dentists.

The market has changed, maybe 10 or 15 years ago you could put an ad in the phonebook, maybe put an ad in the newspaper, do a little direct mail and your practice was set for marketing. It was pretty simple then you didn't have to worry a whole lot about what was going to be effective and what wasn't, there just were not that many options. Now fast forward 5, 10, or 15 years and you see a much more complicated marketing world for your dental practice.

You see most of these traditional forms of marketing are considered "outbound" marketing, where you send your message out to the masses and hope that a certain percentage are looking for a dentist at that given time. Sure it can work, but it can be expensive and not that efficient.

www.ifusedentalmarketing.com

With Internet marketing you can use "inbound" marketing methods that are much more effective and more cost effective. With Internet marketing you can target people that are actively looking for a dentist at that time, you can put your ads in front of people that you know are looking for your dental services. This can be a powerful weapon, if you have a great strategy in place for it.

Just online marketing alone has given you so many different options and choices when it comes to marketing. You probably get calls every day from companies trying to promote you on this site, that site, or another site, or get your practice on the first page of Google. There are so many options today, and you as a dental practice owner or as a dentist may not have the time to look and review all these options and know which is best. Trying to do this can result in wasting a lot of money if you choose the wrong things, or becoming frustrated with the whole model to the point where you don't think online marketing is going to work for your practice, but there is a major problem if that happens.

It's absolutely critical for your practice to be online, and it's not good enough anymore just to be online. You have to be found and you have to be chosen online because guess what, you're not the only dental practice in town. Your competitors are doing online marketing and they may even be hiring local marketing agencies to promote themselves online.

Let me be blunt (I am good at this) if you do not have a plan to make your practice more visible online, then prepare to become irrelevant.

Really what we have here is that Google is the new phonebook. It has taken the place of every day local consumers trying to find local businesses. Instead of going into the closet and picking up a phonebook, they are going to the computer, they are going to their laptop or their mobile device.

www.ifusedentalmarketing.com

I believe that understanding who your patients are is probably the most important factor in doing successful marketing of any kind. If you don't know who your target market is, then there is no way that you can effectively market your practice.

I like to use statistics to help design some of our local marketing strategies. I talk to dental clients on a daily basis, we talk a lot about the facts and we are able to make decisions based on what the facts are in the marketplace. Here are some shocking facts about local online marketing and should help you understand why we believe that this is so critical for our clients:

- 97% of consumers that use the Internet, use it when searching for local products and services (BIA/Kelsey)
- 93% of online research starts with a search engine (buseinss2community)
- There will be over 140 billion <u>local intent</u> searches in 2014 (BIA/Kelsey)
- 95% of smartphone users have looked for local information (Google/Ipsos OTX MediaCT)
- 98% of searchers chooses a business that is on the first page of a search engine (BIA/Kelsey)
- 77% of smart phone users contact a business after looking for local information (Google/Ipsos OTX MediaCT)
- 59% of mobile users who look for local information visit the business on the same day (Google/Ipsos OTX MediaCT)
- 7 out of 10 consumers are more likely to use a local business if it has information available on a social media site (comScore)
- 70% of adult Internet users in the US are now active on at least one social network (mediapost)
- 71% of consumers that receive a quick response to a complaint on social media said they would recommend that company to others (business2community)

www.ifusedentalmarketing.com

- 56% of Google searches have local intent (comScore)
- 88% of consumers consult online reviews before they purchase local services (BrightLocal)
- 88% of consumers trust online reviews as much as personal recommendations (BrightLocal)

Health Specific Marketing Stats:

- 40% of consumers say that information found on social media affects their health decisions (medcitynews)
- 22% of parents use Facebook to seek medical answers online (Mashable)
- 20% of parents use YouTube for medical help (Mashable)
- Online searches for health information is the 3rd most popular online activity (pewInternet)
- 30% of patients say their choice of a dentist is greatly influenced by the quality of a practice's website (Futuredontics)
- Over 70% of consumers are influenced by customer reviews when choosing a dentist (Futuredontics)

These statistics may shock some of you and others may know this, but are uncertain on how to take action. This book is going to help with that.

Google at this time, is the number one place for local searches, so we're going to be talking a lot in this book about Google. You can see that it's critically important to be there.

You probably noticed that I showed a few stats about mobile. Mobile is having the largest increase in usage that we have seen in local marketing ever! You can't ignore mobile usage by your potential new patients, in fact I bet that almost 40% of your website traffic now is coming from mobile devices. You have to design you marketing around mobile and make sure that you are catering to these potential new patients.

www.ifusedentalmarketing.com

If you have studied dental marketing at all, you know that most people like their dental practice to be within 10-15 miles of their house. There are certainly exceptions to that rule, but that's kind of a standard rule that everybody goes by. Now think about mobile devices and how their GPS features allow marketing companies to serve ads based on their location. There are unlimited possibilities in mobile marketing for dental practices!

There is also another way that the Internet influences your new patient counts – online reviews. As you saw from the couple of stats on the previous page, people are looking at your reviews online prior to even calling you. I call this the silent killer, because you may be losing out on new patients and you will never know it. There's no real way to track that, so it's really important when we work with dental clients to ensure that if we are going to drive all this traffic to them, and we are going to get them showing up high on search engines we need to also make sure they have a good online reputation. Sure, you may have good reviews on your website, but who doesn't? You need to get your great reviews out on independent review sites like Google, Yelp, CitySearch and more. If done correctly you can put your great reviews to work for you and make you drastically stand out from your competition.

This book will take you by the hand and show you step-by-step, topic by topic, and tool by tool what you really need to know in order to dominate Local Marketing the easiest way possible, using the most effective tools and in the shortest time ever.

Well it's time to dominate Local Marketing guys. I know you will love this training guide a lot.

To Your Success,

Chris Pistorius
iFuse Dental Marketing

www.ifusedentalmarketing.com

P.S. I'd like to invite you to download a free copy of my exclusive Dental Marketing Ideas Report (a $47 value, free). As an added bonus you'll also get a free subscription to my email only newsletter where I reveal my latest tips, tricks and online marketing strategies. You can do that right now at: http://ifusedentalmarketing.com/bookoffer.

www.ifusedentalmarketing.com

Chapter 1
What is Local Marketing?

In Offline Marketing, "Local Marketing can generally refer to any marketing techniques a localized business, in any industry, uses to market itself to the area it operates in." (Wikipedia)

In Online Marketing, Local Marketing can generally refer to any online marketing techniques that a local business, in any industry, uses to market itself online to the area it operates in.

Local marketing is mostly used by small businesses like local dental practices, but franchise businesses also use local marketing to promote themselves around their specific location. This holds true for dental practices with multiple locations.

A local company uses specific marketing strategies to engage new and potential patients related to their specific community. Transferring that same marketing activity to the online marketing world may bring some outstanding results that can easily surpass those offline marketing activities.

A huge percentage of a dental practices patients search online to know about their services. Those practices can complement their offline business strategies with highly effective online marketing strategies.

Local Marketing provides you with the ability to understand your patient's behaviors and purchasing habits a lot more, because you can know more about your patients online than you can know just by their coming into your practice.

You can use online channels like your website, mobile applications, social media, local search and emails to attract local patients which makes it more power for influencing your potential new patients.

There are four key elements that you need to be aware of when immersing your practice into the Local Marketing world: Segmentation, Media, Messaging and Measurement.

Segmentation: This defines how one group of patients is distinguished from another group of patients. It also refers to "who" you are going to target.

Media: This determines "how" you will deliver your message. It shows what type of media you are using to communicate with your audience like website, mobile applications, social media, local search, emails, etc.

Messaging: This defines "what" you are communicating. These messages are directed to the local population, rather than the mass market. It establishes what you should say to your audiences and in which manner you should convey those messages to turn your audience into patients.

Measurement: This is essential for evaluating your marketing efforts and measuring your results. Positive results can show you how good you are at satisfying the needs of your patients.

Local marketing is an endless process instead of a campaign or event that will end after a fixed time. If you have the correct approach and do it right, it will always give you the highest return of your marketing investment.

How is Local Marketing generally used on the web?

In the online marketing world you can use online marketing strategies to do local marketing so you can build your brand awareness in your neighborhood.

It is all about how you can reach, know and interact with your audience as much as you can. Here are a few online media channels normally used to target local audiences.

Local Website: Local patients normally get excited when their favorite store where they usually go to purchase their goods, has a website showing their products and services. It's a lot easier for a customer to plan with the use of a webpage where is he going to buy stuff before going there.

Having a very informative and constantly updated website will be a great help to your target audience. The majority of people feel too lazy to call sometimes, it's just easier and more fun for them to go online and browse a website.

Local Social Media: People hang out a lot more on social media networks than on a website, and that's where you should establish your presence as well. I have no words to explain how much time, money and effort social media has invested on behalf of local businesses.

The number of followers, likes, shares, reviews, comments, retweets and any other social action shows the interest of your audience in your products. Responding and engaging other social media users is a good way to show that you care about your audience and business.

Local Search: Is your website listed by your location and the local market it serves? Are the keywords and descriptions you used for the search engines used by those people who are searching for a business like yours in a specific area, for example 'Dentist in Shepparton' and 'Pediatric Dentist in Orange County'?

It is amazing the fact that you can target your audience directly by positioning your practice in front of them with the use of Search engines. It has been proven that ranking at the top of the search engines for local terms can be challenging, depending on the competition in your local market.

And the greatest thing is that just a few of your local competitors know about it, which puts you in a unique position to "Steal" their patients by using the Internet.

Local Mobile: The time has come when every single thing created to be used on a desktop computer has to be optimized for mobile devices. If you don't go mobile you will certainly be missing out on a great deal of new patients.

If browsing a website is fun using your laptop or your desktop computer, imaging doing it from your cellphone. If cellphones are in people's pockets and hands, imagine how often they would be able to check out your business.

Local Lead Generation: I have seen how important and trusted Cost per Action websites offer to pay $10 to $20 for every new lead generated on behalf of a business. But in our training we will show you how to get that almost free.

THE ULTIMATE GUIDE TO INTERNET MARKETING FOR DENTISTS

Having your local patients in a contact list is one of the greatest things you will ever do on behalf of the ongoing success of your business. List Building is the greatest Internet marketing strategy ever, and you can even do it locally.

Chapter 2

Why Local Marketing For Dentists?

Amazing Benefits:

Credibility: Having your practices' local presence everywhere on the web will increase your business' authenticity on the web.

If you place your practice on the web with images, physical address and valuable information about your dental services; viewers will rely on your local listings more than other traditional listings.

According to the NDA Group report, about 57% of online users browse online but they buy offline.

Stronger access to local market: You can take advantage of local marketing by having a direct connection with your patients and community. That will maximize the chance to gain additional and future opportunities.

You can also refer the services of other local dentists that offer complementary services. In turn, they will come back to you with extra-added benefits, because other local businesses in your communities will refer you to their patients.

Brand loyalty: A really high level of customer service and the creation of top quality products will help you to build your brand in your local community really well. Make sure to offer quality and provide the best services to your local patients.

You can also use social media for communication and engagement with your patients. Social media can be the best way to gather brand loyalty for your practice if you update it on a regular basis.

Accessibility for mobile searchers: If your website is registered in local directories and has a mobile optimized layout then your viewers can easily find and navigate it. This will add an extra advantage over your competition.

Millions, if not all mobile devices have applications which help the customer find any business near them. These applications will help you get a large amount of potential patients coming through your practices' doors.

Easy to implement: Complexity is a word that is disappearing over the web nowadays. One of the strongest visions of any service or product on the web is to make it as easy as possible for the user.

The same can be said about Local Marketing. You will be amazed how much time, money and effort important companies are spending to create the greatest local marketing tools ever that are 100% free to you or at least a fraction of the real cost.

Targeting and personalization: You will get extremely targeted patients for your services because you will know who they are, where they come from and what they like.

You can classify your patients on their demographic profile like age, gender, buying habits, geographic location, income level, occupation, hobbies and interests. You can do almost anything on the web.

Increase revenue: How much do you usually spend on local marketing activities around your local business area? How much do you think you can get doing it on the web and way faster? With just a few clicks.

That alone will save you a good amount of money. But the principal idea of targeting a lot more of your local patients a lot faster is leading them to visit your office more often. And that is also possible.

Analytics: Analytics allows you to see who is looking for your services, when they last checked out your website and where they were online previously. That's something really hard to do offline.

These statistics will allow you to adjust your marketing plan accordingly. You can completely monitor your social media and website activities. All these things have a positive effect on your productivity.

Free traffic: Yeah, that's right, you will get a lot of free local-customer traffic to your website when you submit it to local directories.

Google states that 40% of mobile queries are related to local business searches. Several search engines also have local directories where you can submit your listing too.

Channel engagement: The less traffic your competitor's website gets, the more opportunity you have to engage those patients, promote your products and services in your community and increase your revenue streams.

As you know local engagement is key to increasing your revenue. People will remember you because you are there constantly reminding them that your awesome offer is about to expire.

Shocking Facts:

Here are some amazing eye opening facts that will show you why you have to use Local Marketing to market your Business. (LinkedIn)

74% of Internet **users perform local searches.**	
	More than 100 MILLION PEOPLE a month use Google Maps from mobile phones to find business information.
66% of American's use online local search, like Google local search to locate local businesses.	
	61% of local searches result in purchases.
54% of Americans have substituted the Internet and local search for phone books.	
	Microsoft has claimed that 53% of mobile searches on Bing are local in nature.
82% of local searches follow up offline via an in-store visit, phone call or purchase.	
	Nearly ONE in TWO shoppers for local products and services are using their smartphones.

Without a mobile presence, you are essentially neglecting or potentially insulting HALF of your target demographic.	
	As much as 43% of Google Search traffic has local content.

Data like this makes it clear there is a lot of money to be made with Local Marketing. And while lots of people might be talking about it, very few can really teach you how to productively use Local Marketing on behalf of your practice.

Chapter 3

Dental Marketing Power Tools

Power Tool #1: LocalVox

LocalVox is a local and social media platform that helps you market your practice online. With LocalVox you can promote your practice across a network of publishers, social media, mobile, search engine and on your website - and all these are as easy as using your email account.

LocalVox saves you time with a single partner and provides solutions for local Internet marketing. It drives better results for your local business with an all in one marketing platform. LocalVox saves you money with pricing that you can afford.

There are so many online marketing channels, so it becomes very hard to keep your business on top. LocalVox puts your business in front of your target audience everywhere online.

Power Tool #2: Sweetiq

If your patients don't find you when they search, you might as well not exist, so Sweetiq is an all-in-one location based online marketing platform for local businesses, brands, and franchises.

A local and organic keyword tracker finds out the keywords that you can use to compete in local search. You can track your patients' activities on twitter and check-in on foursquare.

Sweetiq provides local competitor analysis for your business that monitors your local and organic keyword rankings on Google, Bing and Yahoo. It also tells you the online directories, social media profiles, blogs and websites that would help you to improve your local business rankings.

Local business listing management from Sweetiq discovers where your business is listed online, finds the gaps and gives you 100% local search coverage. It also identifies inaccuracies or inconsistencies and fixes them in a single click.

THE ULTIMATE GUIDE TO INTERNET MARKETING FOR DENTISTS

Sweetiq reviews, monitors, and listens where and what your patients are talking about your business and products.

Power Tool #3: MOZ Local

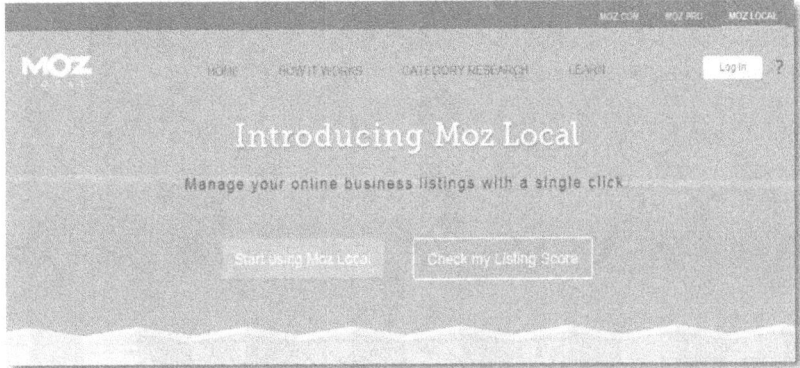

MOZ Local is designed for local businesses and businesses who manage multiple local businesses. With MOZ Local you can easily manage your online listing, all you need to do is upload your business information with a click and it notifies you if any issues arise.

You can establish a consistent business listing in directories and popular websites with MOZ Local. MOZ Local emails you reminders to update your listings and re-verify your local business listings information to establish correct and consistent listings.

The Category Research tool of MOZ Local helps you choose the right search engine categories for your local business. It also provides transparent reports of your listings and it is the only self-service location data management software that lists your local business with all five major U.S. data aggregators.

Power Tool #4: AllLocal

AllLocal was launched in 2008 to target individual needs of local markets. You need a unique approach to generate local traffic for your multi-location local business with a strong online reputation.

AllLocal resolves this problem. The AllLocal online platform decreases the required time to manage your practices' local search presence.

It handles all the factors of local search like address validation, listing optimization, and Google listings; it also tracks online reviews about your local business. It offers a customized location navigator, powerful bulk edit functionality and performance reporting.

AllLocal also provides online reports and the monitoring status of your listings that will help you to determine the ROI that your local search listing will generate.

Power Tool #5: Balihoo

Balihoo is the premier provider of local marketing automation with cloud-based platform that gets result for local markets. Balihoo is automated marketing software for personalized local campaigns.

Balihoo drives relevant leads at local level and make sure that your local audience can find your services according to categories. Balihoo website templates are designed to drive local traffic.

It also helps national brands to get leads with online forms, focused call-to-action message and trackable local calls at local level. Your mobile websites are also optimized for search results and conversion because of built-in adaptive design with Balihoo.

Balihoo gives you easy to use templates, so just by adding your information you are all set with a great local marketing weapon in your hands. You will get real time analytics by individual location if you are running a multi-location based local marketing campaign.

Power Tool #6: SproutLoud

You want to generate your brand awareness and drive sales to your practice form your local market, so Sprout Loud is here to help you with customized local online marketing. SproutLoud uses Local Search, Local PPC, Triggered Communications, Email Marketing, Direct Mail, Social Media, Mobile Sites, Review Monitoring and local media buying services to market your business locally.

Email marketing send brand-approved emails to your targeted audience that will convert your audience into patients.

It generates brand-approved paid search and ad campaigns with your business information; your audiences will find you online and make their purchase immediately.

Social media will help to increase and build your fan base which will drive more people to your practice.

Power Tool #7: SignPost

SignPost will feature your practice on every website and mobile application, including Google, Facebook, Yahoo, Yelp and many more.

SignPost is the simplest and most effective way to get found by your local patients. It will automatically update information on directories and social media sites to make you stand out from the crowd.

SignPost automatically advertises your local business to your new patients and targeted audiences. It will turn your local online advertising into real revenue by promoting your special deals.

You can engage your customer with Social media channels and email marketing. You can also remarket to your old and potential patients to get them back.

Power Tool #8: RioSEO

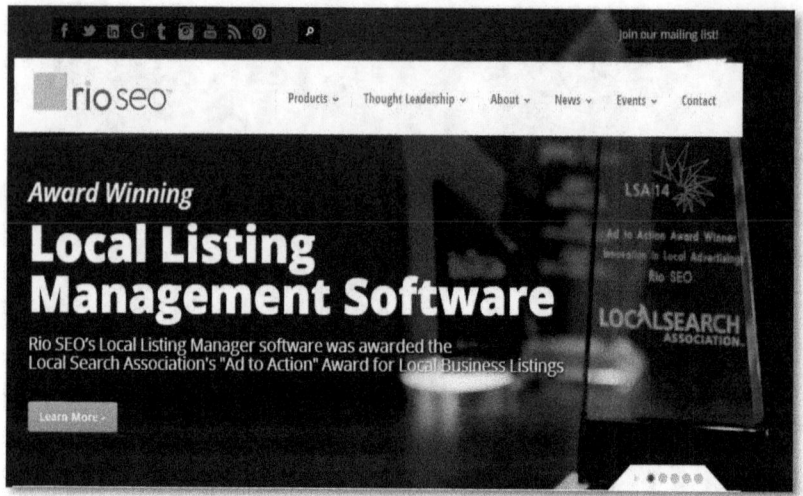

You are a local marketer or have multi-location businesses and want software to optimize your local search, website. You can go for RioSEO tools for SEO automation, Content marketing, Local search, reporting and competitive analysis.

Local search business listing management increases accuracy of your local business listings and organic local search presence.

You can easily manage conversions tools and data with Local SEO optimized landing pages, which maximizes the user experience and provides you with the detailed analytics report according to location.

You can target your local market with Local SEO; it will find your search engine presence in Organic Search and Local Map Listings. You can optimize your local business listings for consistency on Google+ Local, Yahoo Local and Bing Places.

Power Tool #9: Kenshoo

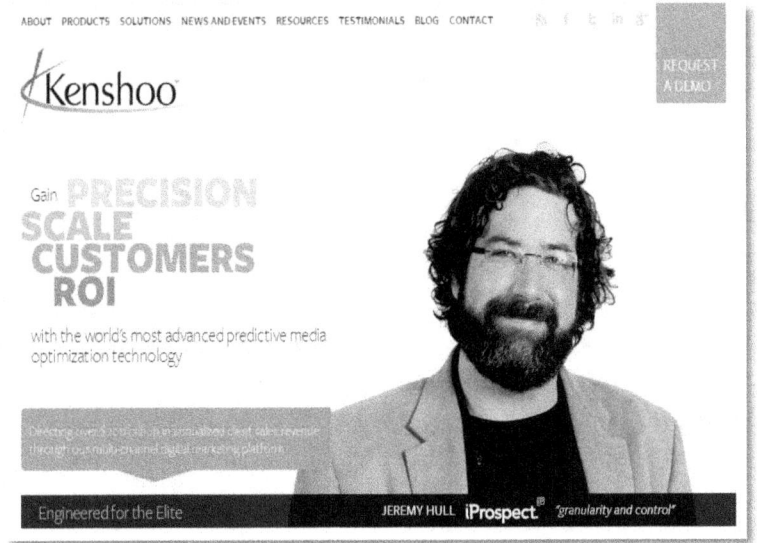

Kenshoo local is an extendable platform to manage local marketing campaigns for individual stores, dealers, agencies and other local business. Kenshoo Local's tailored functionality will allow you to successfully manage your local search, places and directories listings.

It's on-boarding & campaign management uses profile wizard, Campaign Template, Cross-Profile Advanced Search and Radius Geo-targeting that launches new local online marketing campaigns with an easy-to-follow guide, helping you to access saved templates keywords and ad copy for advertising in local markets and target your local audience within a specified distance.

Kenshoo local manages your bids and goals with tools that are designed to optimize and scale. It automatically rolls over your unused budget with pre-set rules and an optimized search program to drive more leads to meet your business needs.

Power Tool #10: ElementsLocal

You are running a multi-location practice and want to promote it locally; ElementsLocal will help you deliver the power of your brand to your local patients.

ElementsLocal generates more leads, broadcasts your brand awareness, and enhances the presence of your online marketing. It includes consistent monitoring and tweaking to establish satisfactory results.

It uses Email marketing, social media Marketing and Local Search to empower your business strategy.

ElementsLocal automatically submits your franchise locations to search engines and directories and allows franchisees to update certain content. It also shows mobile friendly websites to patients who are using mobile devices.

Chapter 4

How to Do Dental Marketing the Right Way

In this step-by-step process I will show you the greatest 7 strategies to get the most out of Local Marketing on the web on behalf of your dental practice. I will show you the easiest, fastest and cheapest ways to apply these strategies.

Those strategies area: Local Website, Local Search, Local Marketing on Social Media, Local Marketing on Mobiles, and Local Lead Generation.

Strategy #1: Local Website

I'm sure you didn't know that there is an absolutely awesome website somewhere on the web, completely related to your business topic and ready to plug in and start using it right away.

Well that's because someone very talented has taken the time to apply several awesome Local Marketing tricks on them and is offering them to you for a fraction of the cost and even free.

Today creating a website has become extremely easy, really.

What we recommend you do is use what is called a Responsive WordPress theme for Local Marketing. "Responsive" means your website can be viewed on absolutely any device of any size.

Responsive WordPress themes are the future made the present for extraordinary business websites. With a WordPress theme you can do almost anything with your website by just installing a plug-in.

There are awesome places to find really nice Dental WordPress Themes, ready to be displayed on every single computer device, at the same time.

You can Google it. Just Google Dental WordPress theme and you will find a lot of great templates to use.

Themeforest.net is one of the greatest places to find some really nice Responsive WordPress themes especially for your practice. You just search for what you need and there you will find multiple options.

InkThemes.com has an extraordinary collection of Dental WordPress themes as well. They will even show you some live examples of the Theme and by resizing your browser checking these options here you will be able to check out how responsive it is.

WordPress.org gives you a lot free WordPress themes, itself. They will even give you access to free theme samples of the paid themes services for testing purposes.

You can also visit other websites listed on Google to find some awesome ideas and many more free business theme samples to try out.

As you can see, there is plenty of help for you to create a really nice Professional Dental Website, fast, quick and easy. And training is something to worry about even less because there is plenty of it.

You can find plenty of videos on YouTube and even those WordPress Theme Vendors have their own training on how to install it. Even your hosting company will have a personalized way to install WordPress with just a few clicks.

Strategy #2: Local Search

Local search is the use of specialized Internet search engines that allow users to submit geographically constrained searches against a structured database of local business listings.

Typical local search queries include not only information about "what" the site visitor is searching for (such as keywords, a business category, or the name of a consumer product) but also "where" information, such as a street address, city name, postal code, or geographic coordinates like latitude and longitude.

Examples of local searches include "dentists in Denver", "Boise cosmetic dentist", and "Cleveland teeth whitening".

So, in other words, here we will be looking to get our business presence in the top of the search engine results so our local clients can find our business once they search for a topic directly related to our business.

There are a lot of Search Engines used by people to find answers to their needs and questions. But the most important of all are Google, Yahoo and Bing.

- **Google My Business:**

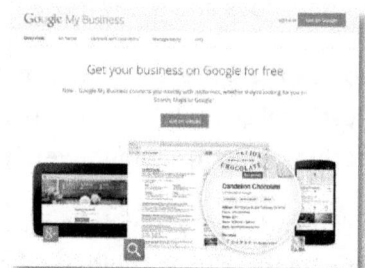

Google has recently launched what is called Google My Business. I've gotta tell you it's just absolutely great.

Google My Business consists of a multi-layer platform, which connects you directly with patients, whether they're looking for you on Search, Maps or Google+.

You just need to create your Google Offline Business Account, which is free by clicking on Get on Google. Of course, you will need to have a Gmail account already created in order to have access to this service as well.

If you already have created any Google Maps or Google Places account, login with those same details and make sure everything is updated.

Once logged in you will able to create a new page. Google will take your current location at every step of the process, because logically you are trying to create a Google Business Page in your local area.

THE ULTIMATE GUIDE TO INTERNET MARKETING FOR DENTISTS

After choosing your Business Type, you will be able to submit the name of your business, and if you don't find your business listed which probably is what is going to happen, then you can click on "Let me enter the full business details"

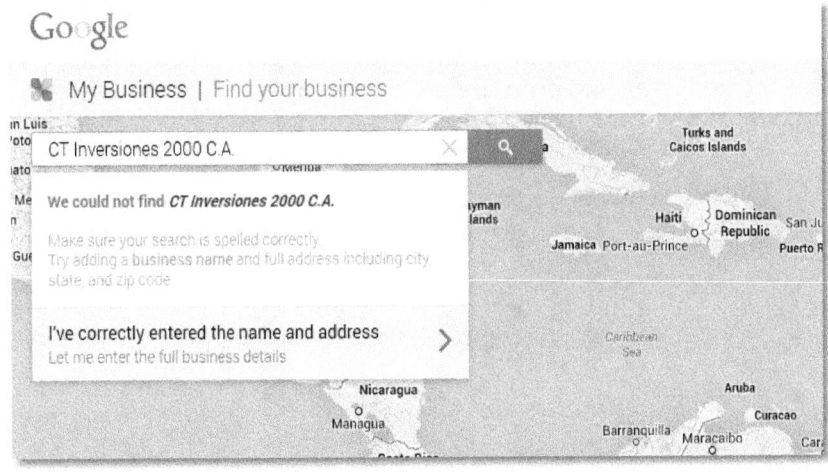

Then you will submit all of your Offline Business information with all the details.

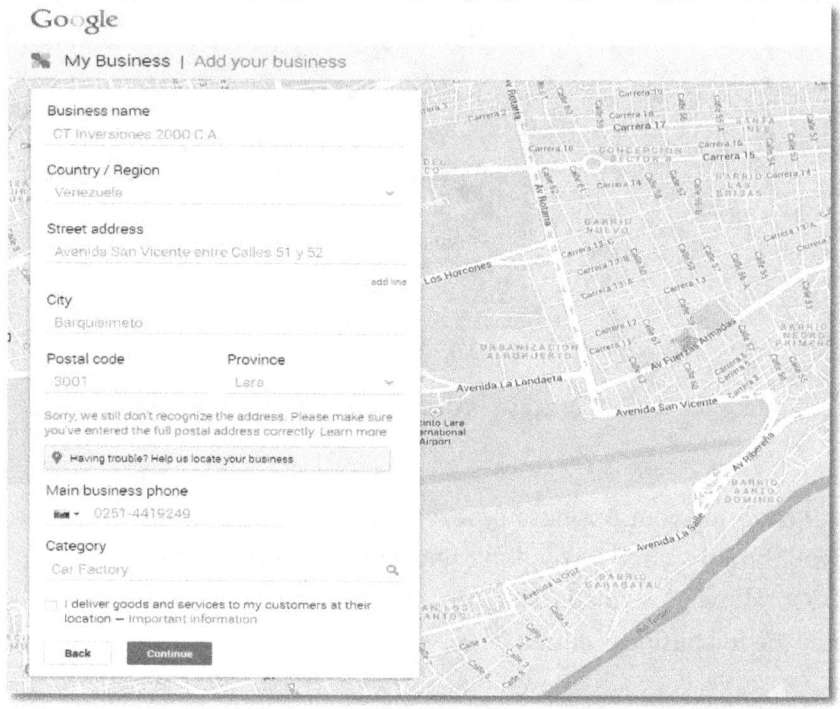

Google will even give you the ability to find exactly where your offline business is located. You just need to search on the map where it is exactly located, drag and drop the red pin on top of your business and click on "done".

THE ULTIMATE GUIDE TO INTERNET MARKETING FOR DENTISTS

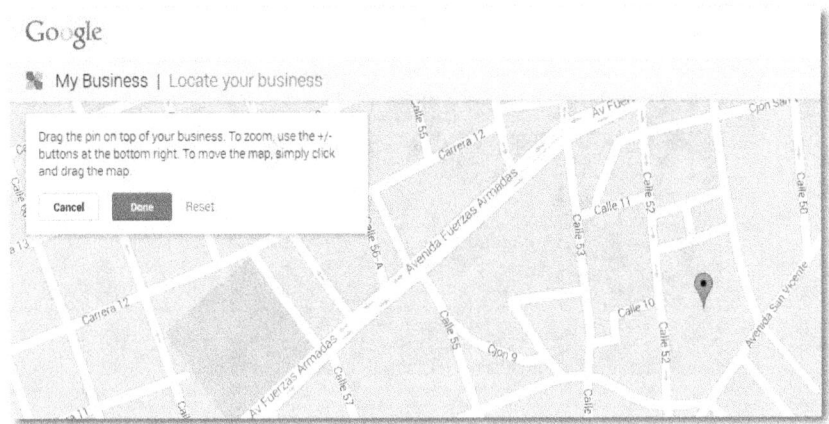

Then after clicking on continue, you will be asked if you are authorized to manage this business and if you agree the terms of service.

Then you will need to verify your association with this practice with a verification code that will be sent to the postal address you have just inserted into your business Information.

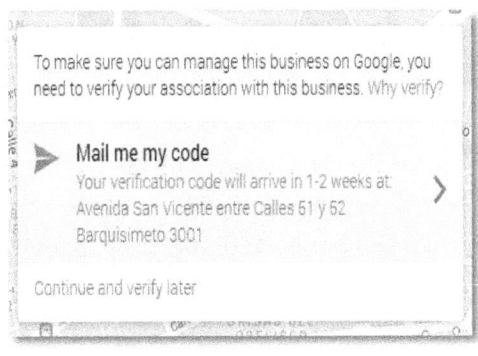

Then after that confirmation requirement, you will be lead to your brand new Google Business Account, which is connected to all the amazing tools Google has created for your business, which is absolutely amazing.

www.ifusedentalmarketing.com

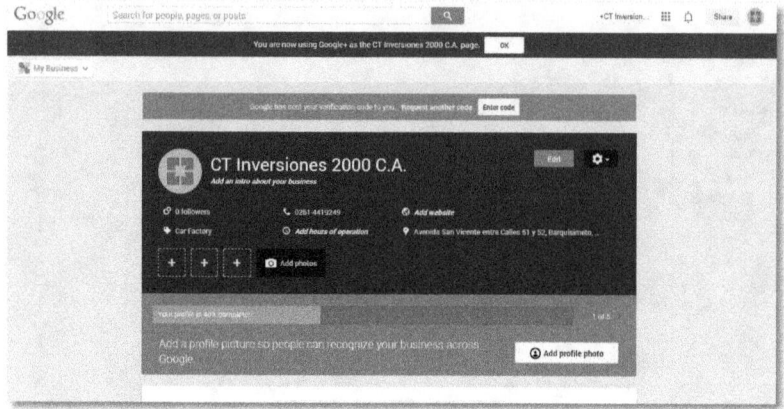

Let me give you 4 very important pieces of advice to consider using Google My Business:

1. You must do every single thing Google asks you to do throughout the process.
2. Inside your Google's Business Page dashboard, by clicking on Edit, you will be able to add a lot more important information - you must add every single thing there, too.
3. We strongly advise you to use 100% accurate information, you must use your real Business name (not a keyword), updated business address, real contact info, your actual business hours, real business picture and a really professional and descriptive introduction, etc.
4. We advise you to check if there are other Google Business Pages for the exact same company, this is not good at all. Clicking on the settings you will be able to see all pages listed, just go inside of the duplicated one, click on edit, and going down you will find the "Delete this Page" link.

Finally, I would like you to know the principal Ranking Factors of your Google Business Page

- ✓ **Accurate and Optimized Business Information:** all of your business information should be completely filled and accurate in

all places: Google Products, Website, Local Listings, etc.
- ✓ **Real followers:** the greater the number of real followers from your local area your business has the higher the ranking potential your business will get for that same audience related to your local business.
- ✓ **Posts frequencies:** consistent updates will tell people you are alive and that you are always trying to offer new content to your audience
- ✓ **Followers engagement:** another sign of being alive is your followers' engagement. There is no point having a great deal of real followers for your local business Google listing if no one is having real and constant interaction with your business.
- ✓ **Reviews:** reviews are an extremely important feature Google My Business is offering as well. Google organizes reviews by score as well, and besides registering these reviews inside of Google's platform, Google has also the ability to retrieve and store those reviews from other websites. Something that is offering real value to other people will surely be picked up by Google to be on top.
- ✓ **Citations:** with this we mean that your NAP (Local Business Name, Local Business Address and your Local Business Phone number) should be everywhere on the web. We can call this Off-Page SEO.

Small Business Yahoo:

Yahoo is not far behind when it comes to Local Marketing Services for Local Businesses.

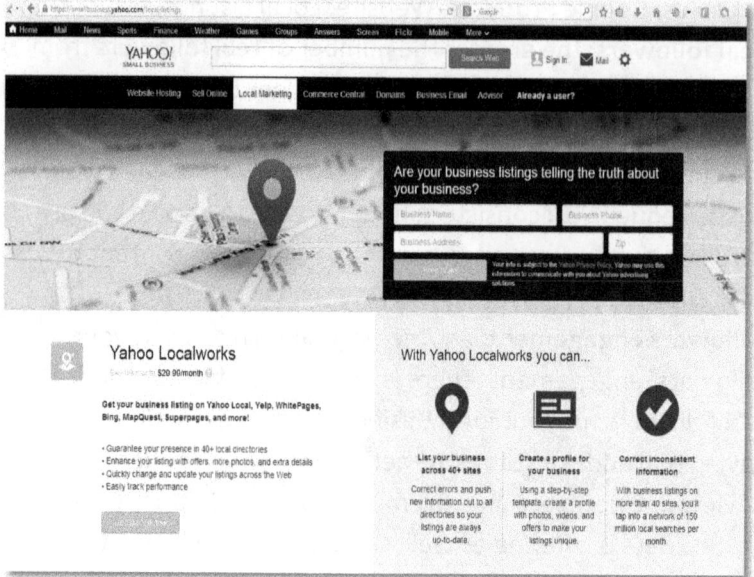

Yahoo has introduced an absolutely awesome service called Yahoo Localworks.

With this service you will be able to get your business listing on Yahoo Local, Yelp, WhitePages, Bing, MapQuest, Superpages, and more!

But one of the greatest services guarantees your presence in 40+ local directories, which is just awesome.

This submission to local directories will skyrocket your top ranking potential on Google and on any other search engine as well.

Besides all this, with Yahoo you will be able to tap into a network of 150 million local searches per month.

Bing Places:

Bing is actually offering the same service for local business.

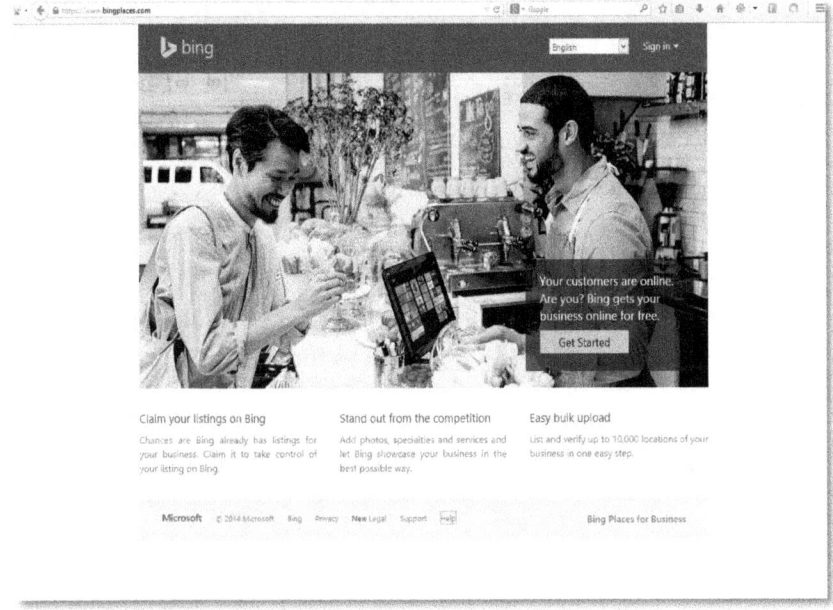

"Bing Places for Business is a free service that allows you to add or claim your business listing on Bing and be found by millions of Bing users searching online. Claiming your listing allows you to take control of your business information online and enrich it with content like photos, cuisine & menu URLs, phone numbers, and other relevant information."

"This information can help Bing users to learn more about your products and services as well as how to contact you if they desire to initiate a transaction with your business." (Bing)

You can find the same services offered by other search engines as well. It's a matter of searching a little bit and establishing your local business at the place your patients constantly go to, to search for something on the web.

Strategy #3: Local Marketing on Social Media

Social Media has invested a great deal of money, time and effort into positioning any local business on their respective platforms a lot easier every time and with a great percentage of productivity.

Facebook:

Facebook offers some awesome services especially for Local Businesses. The two most important services for local business are the Facebook Page and Facebook Advertising.

- ✓ **Facebook Page**

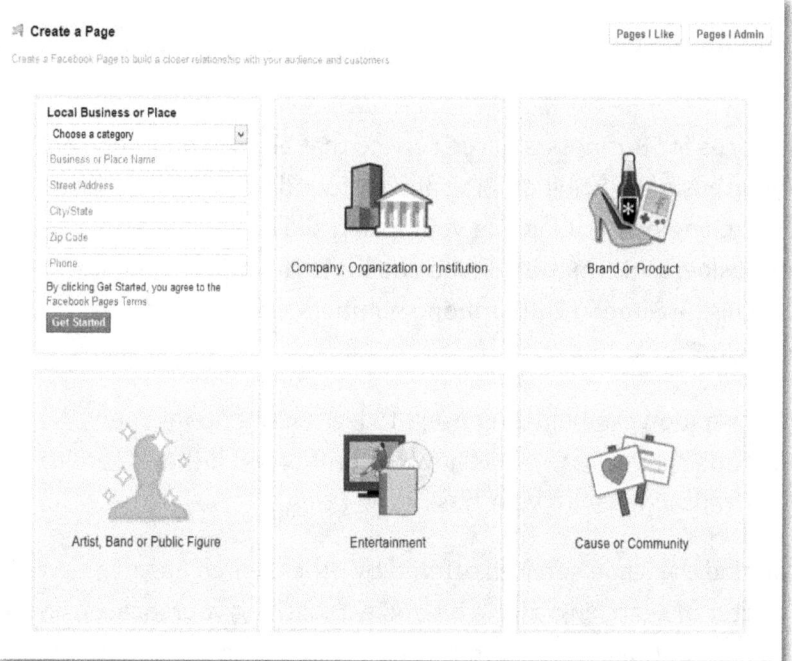

On Facebook you will be able to create a Facebook Page especially for your practice. Facebook will supply you with all the necessary tools adapted to your practice needs to reach as many of your local patients as possible.

Something awesome about creating a Facebook Page for practice is what is called the Graph Search:

As you can see, Facebook fixes the search results to show Local Places for people searching for a term, and that's very important for your Local Business Facebook Page get relevant visitors that are 100% free.

✓ **Facebook Advertising**

Besides getting free traffic to your Facebook Page from the Graphic Search. Facebook also gives you the ability to advertise to as many people as you want from your local area by what is called Pay per Click Advertising.

Facebook has built an amazing Advertising Platform where you will be able to advertise almost anything you want in several different ways.

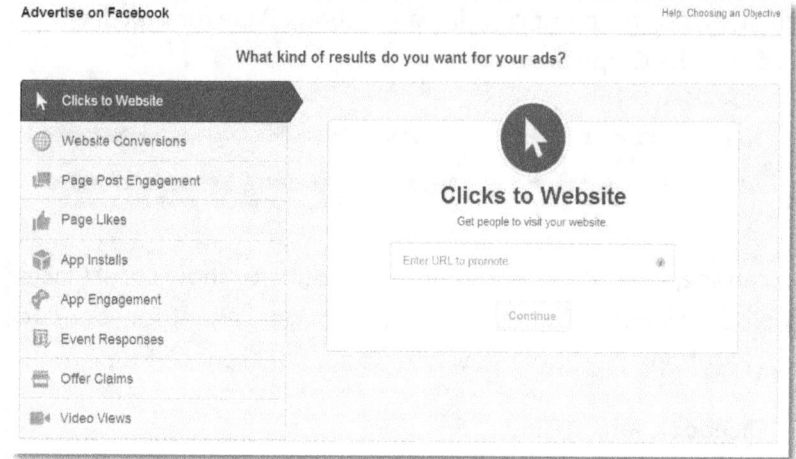

And when I say, "advertise to as many people as you want from your local area" I do mean it. I think the fact that you can even advertise to Facebook Users living in a small suburb of your city is enough reason for you to be shocked.

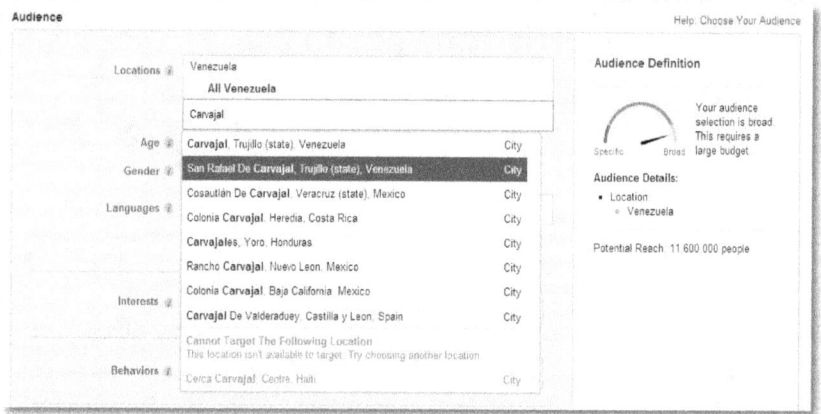

Twitter:

Twitter also offer some amazing online advertising tools for local businesses. As with Facebook, Twitter gives your business the option of creating a Twitter Page as well as Advertising on their sponsored sections.

THE ULTIMATE GUIDE TO INTERNET MARKETING FOR DENTISTS

✓ **Twitter Page**

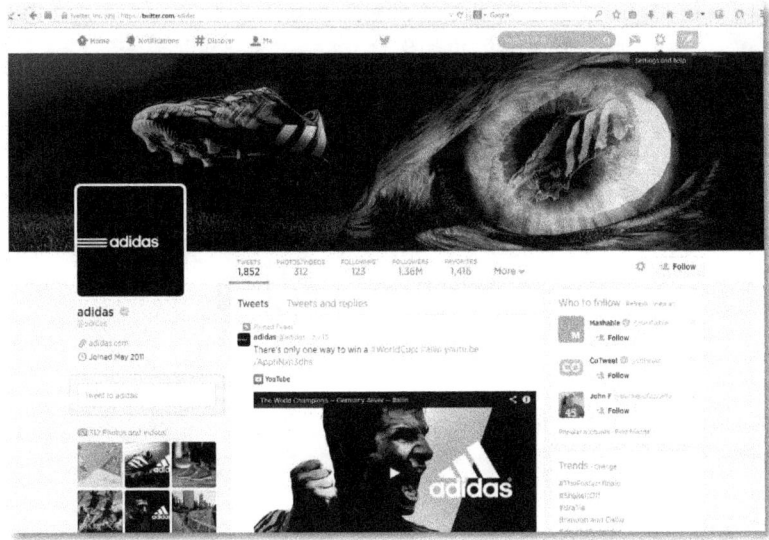

Creating a Twitter Page for your business is just as easy as creating a basic twitter page, you just need to use your Local Business Details to create the account.

Similar to Facebook, with twitter you will have a personalized URL identifying your Twitter Page (https://twitter.com/yourcompanyname). Something that can really boost your brand over the web.

✓ **Twitter Advertising**

Twitter has a wide collection of Advertising options as well.

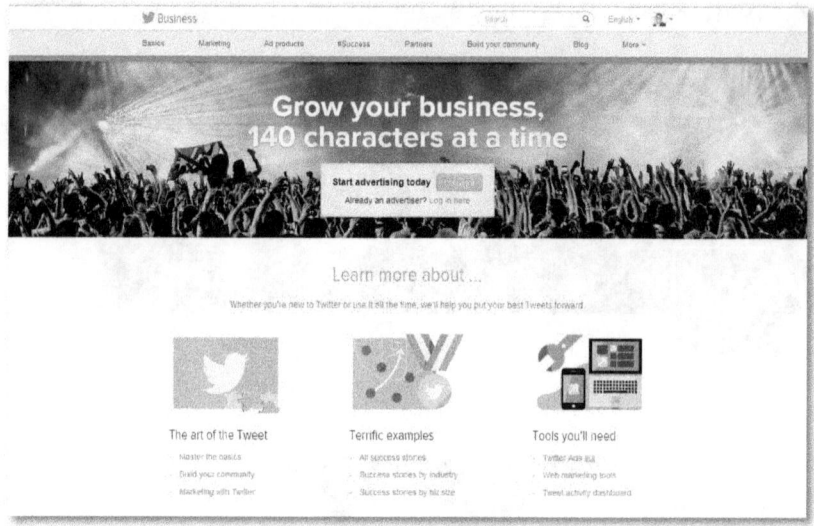

Besides giving you the tools, they will even provide you great examples of success stories you could easily clone and apply.

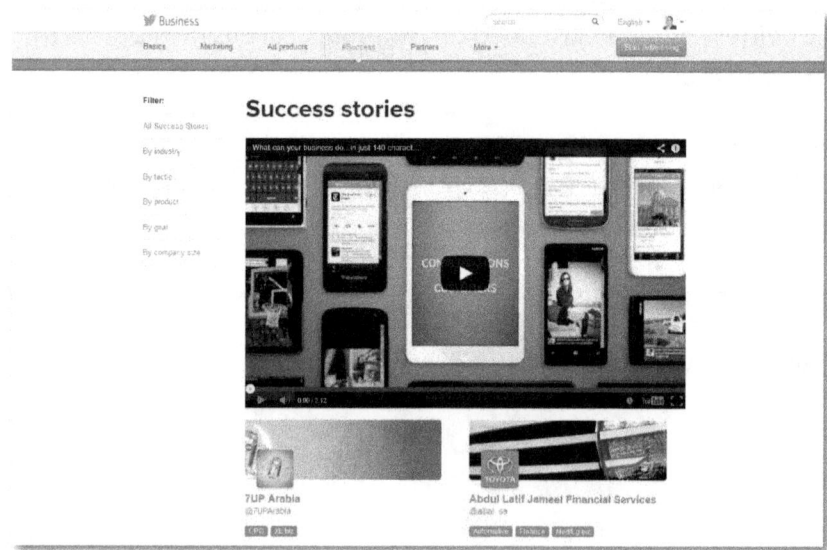

THE ULTIMATE GUIDE TO INTERNET MARKETING FOR DENTISTS

Pinterest:

Since it started, Pinterest has been doing wonders on social media. They also cater to businesses and have a very nice social experience for your practice ready for you to enjoy.

- ✓ **Pinterest Business Pages**

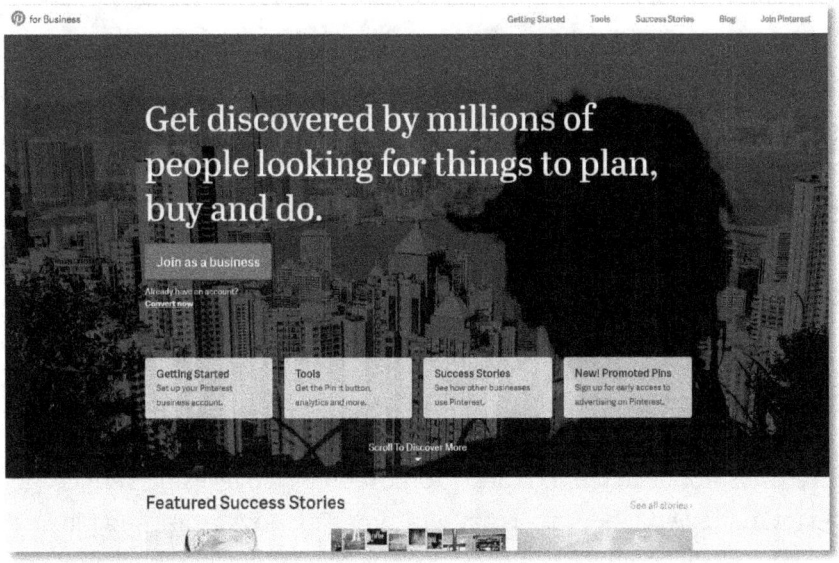

You can freely join as a business directly, or if you already have a Basic Pinterest account you created previously for your business, you can just convert it.

Pinterest offers you a special place to show you wonderful success stories people are actually experiencing by using Pinterest for their Business purposes.

Pinterest is slightly different than other social platforms, because it is a platform based primarily on image sharing. Nevertheless, your audience might be hanging out there as much as other social platforms, so having multiple opportunities to reach them is not exactly bad for your business don't you think?

- ✓ **Pinterest Advertising**

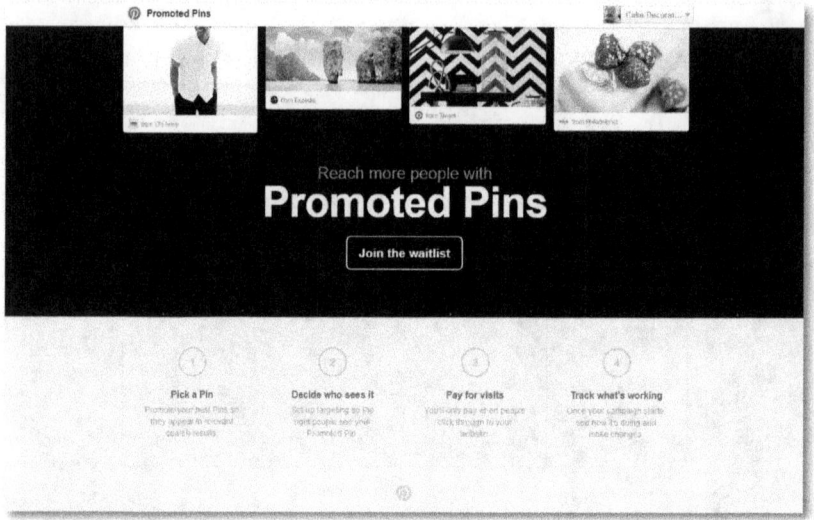

Pinterest is about to launch their Promoted Pins advertising service. And let me tell you, pins are crazy viral, imagine how promoted pins will be. So be ready to check out their service. Maybe it's live right now, so go ahead and check it out right away.

In strategy I didn't include Google+, which is very strong for Local Businesses, and the reason is that Google My Business has included all their amazing tools for local businesses there, including Google+.

So avoid getting confused with Google+ and get the most out of Google+ for your practice by using Google My Business.

Strategy #4: Local Marketing on Mobile

The whole world is on mobile. Even you are on mobile, your offline patients are on mobile, don't your think your practice deserves to be on mobile too?

According to experts on the subject, it has been discovered that if you don't have a Mobile Strategy you can't connect with well over half of your audience!

People check their mobile devices dozens of times a day, so it just makes good sense to get your business in on the non-stop action by going mobile.

Do you realize how volcanically hot Mobile Marketing is getting at this exact moment?

- ✓ The number of mobile devices almost exceeds the number of people on earth
- ✓ One in four online searches is done on a mobile device
- ✓ The average American spends 2 hours a day on his mobile device
- ✓ 40% of users who scan a QR code will buy the product
- ✓ 68% of people use a mobile device to look up a store address
- ✓ 52% of mobile users check the prices of an item online they wish to buy
- ✓ 91% of Smart phone users keep their phone within arm's length
- ✓ 70% of all mobile searches result in an action within an hour
- ✓ 52% of mobile searchers call the Company they are researching
- ✓ 47% of mobile users are more likely to read reviews online for the product

And there are so many ways to get on mobile nowadays, and all of them are automatic and convenient.

You have already applied many of those ways already by applying the first 3 local marketing strategies we have been learning about.

Mobile Website:

If you correctly applied Strategy #1, you have already achieved this extremely important step. A Responsive WordPress Website is the best solution for this.

Having a Responsive WordPress Website will give people the ability to see your practice website from absolutely any device. They can visit your website from their desktop or laptop computer, they can check it out on their table or mobile computer, and they can even check it out on from their mobile phones.

If you have already invested a lot of money on your existing website, there is a way to create a mobile version of it, so mobile users can visit that version instead of the non-mobile version.

There are two ways to do this, you could create a mobile website from scratch. Or you can convert your existing website into a mobile website.

JQMBuilder.com offers an absolutely simple and awesome platform to create your Mobile Website in a matter of minutes.

"JQMBuilder is a powerful online tool that can produce basic professional looking jQuery Mobile Websites in minutes. Its purpose is to provide designers and developers with a tool that can save lots of time when producing jQuery Mobile prototypes." Source

They will train you step by step how to do it by yourself.

If your intention is to create a mobile website by using your existing non-mobile website, there are 2 ways to do it: one works for WordPress websites and one works for Non-WordPress websites.

If you already have a WordPress website installed but it's not responsive, this will be the easiest and fastest way to create a Mobile Website.

The first thing you have to do is to check your site and determine whether or not it is responsive, and to do that you can simply visit your site using the Opera Mobile Emulator.

As you can see, this site is not responsive because it is displayed as if you were on a desktop computer. As is, the text is absolutely impossible to read.

People need to be able to see your website from their mobile devices without having to magnify the interface so they can read your content.

You can convert that non-mobile WordPress website to mobile by installing a plugin called WP Mobile Detector Mobile Plugin.

Make sure to follow every step of the process in order to activate that plugin. After you are done installing and activating the plugin your brand new mobile website will look like this:

Extremely easy don't you think?

You don't have to do anything, what you just did was convert your website into a Responsive website, ready to be accessed with absolutely any mobile device and desktop computer.

Now let me show you how to do the same thing to a non-WordPress website.

For a non-WordPress website, the service we will use is called dudamobile.com. What you will be creating here is a complete Mobile Website but using your existing website.

The process is so simple.

First, you submit the URL of your website.

Secondly, you redesign the mobile website however you want which is optional.

And lastly, you go live. It's that simple. I would say it just doesn't get any easier than that.

Mobile Social Media:

Well, here you don't have to do absolutely anything. For just applying Strategies #2 and #3 you or your practice is already on Mobile with Social Media. That's because all Social Platforms have gone mobile already, which is absolutely brilliant.

THE ULTIMATE GUIDE TO INTERNET MARKETING FOR DENTISTS

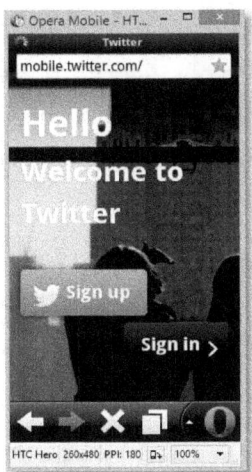

Strategy #5: Local Lead Generation

Lead generation is the practice of soliciting inquiries from potential patients. Building a leads list of your potential patients is key for your local practices' success.

The practice of collecting those local business leads will increase your sales drastically, because the action of a potential customer giving their contact information to be contacted, significantly increases the chances of them becoming a new patient.

Besides that, having a list will give you the option of contacting those potential patients more often, letting them know the great benefits your product or service possess so those potential patients can finally buy your main and even additional services.

But having success with this absolutely awesome local marketing technique will depend on the quality of those leads.

What is a High Quality Local Lead?

For example, if a visitor goes to your website, and fill outs a form to request more information, giving you even a phone number so you can call that visitor back, this is considered a high quality lead, they will be more likely to become a patient.

On the other hand if you decide to build a list of leads based on a subscription list from another company, you will find yourself in the situation of registering low quality leads that are indirectly interested in your product or services.

As you can see, a High Quality Local Lead is a Lead you collect using your own local marketing tools directly and not by alternate ways. So the quality will be assured by the Lead Generation Techniques you apply.

How can we generate High Quality Local Leads?

By "Your Own Local Marketing Tools" we mean the tools you already have learned so far; like your practice website, your practices' social accounts, your practice mobile website if you decided to created it separately from your regular website, etc.

Those places are what you can use to generate High Quality Leads. But there is another very important tool you will use in order to connect it all to your local website, or local social accounts or your local mobile website, and that tool would be a Lead Generation Software program.

There are several lead generation tools on the web. Very Powerful tools you can use in order to collect and build your local lead so you can use it however you want to increase your patient engagement, productivity and revenue really well.

You can use services like: AWeber, GetResponse, MailChimp, IContact, 1ShopingCart, etc.

There are a lot of other services but I strongly advise that you make sure the service is trustworthy and also that is not 100% free. Because those free lead generation services can lead you into big trouble in the future.

Another piece of advice is that you don't have to waste a lot of money on those local lead generation services on the web. You can do it yourself, you don't have to waste your money on this part.

You need to do only 1 thing. And that is sending highly targeted traffic to a local lead capture form. Now let me give you some really cool tricks:

Trick #1: You can insert a lead capture form in the home page of your website, that way all traffic your website gets may potentially lead to a lead capture.

Trick #2: You can sponsor a special local deal promotion, you can ask people to fill out their details on a lead capture page you will send them to and advertise that promotion everywhere.

Trick #3: You can sponsor a patient's personal details update, where you will ask all patients to update all of their personal contact information in exchange for a huge prize which will be randomly delivered to 10 or so participants.

Trick #4: Another cool idea is having a special coupon advertisement, where people have to come to your website, submit their contact information so they can receive that coupon code on their email accounts and then redeem it in under 7 days.

Trick #5: what about creating a special video to show people live about how to use your services, or how other people are using your services. Then you can just have a lead capture page sitting there for them to get access to that content.

Strategy #6: Pay Per Click Marketing

PPC stands for Pay-Per-Click - a popular advertising technique on the Internet. Found on websites, advertising networks, and especially on search engines, PPC advertising involves sponsored links that are typically in the form of text ads. These are usually placed close to search results, where an advertiser pays a particular amount to visitors who click on these links or banners and land on the advertiser's web page.

In essence, PPC advertising is all about bidding for the top or leading position on search engine results and listings. Advertisers do this by buying or bidding on keyword phrases that are relevant to their products or services - the higher the bid, the higher the spot on the search results, the more the people will find the ad (and click on it) to go to their websites (this is why some people call it "keyword auctioning"). Advertisers would then pay the bidding price every time a visitor clicks through the website.

PPC advertising is also known under the following names/variations:

- Pay per placement
- Pay per performance
- Pay per ranking
- Pay per position
- Cost per click (CPC)

PPC advertising is usually done with the following standard procedures:

- ✓ Setting up an account and/or deposit funds.
- ✓ Creating a keyword list.
- ✓ Choosing (and setting up) an account with a PPC search engine.
- ✓ Bidding on the ad placement, including the search result words or phrases.
- ✓ Writing out an ad copy.
- ✓ Setting up the 'landing pages' for your ads.
- ✓ Placing the advertisement in the search engine.

There are many benefits to Pay Per Click advertising, making it an effective way of promoting a dental practice online. Some of them are listed below:

- Get launched immediately. PPC advertisements are implemented very quickly - they can go 'online' within an hour after winning the bid and paying for it.
- Obtain specific, pre-qualified, and quality traffic. PPC provides you with a quality or a well-targeted traffic. Visitors are narrowed down into 'qualified' people who are actually looking for specific products and/or services that you offer - those who are more likely to become a 'lead' (a convert) and complete a transaction (either by buying your product or subscribing to the service that you are offering.
- Widen your reach. PPC advertising provides additional traffic to your site, aside from the natural or "organic" search engines.
- Track your investment. PPC advertising makes use of a tracking system that will determine exactly who comes to the website and what they do once they arrive - the length of their stay on the site and the number of pages (including the actual pages) that they view. These are valuable tools in determining statistics such as return on investment (ROI), acquisition cost-per-visitor, and conversion rates (the percentage of visitors who are converted into patients or leads).

Below are some important things to consider when planning on a pay per click campaign:

1. Know your practice.

Know what are the most important dental services that you offer, as well as the most popular ones (before anything else).

2. Stay within the budget.

Determine your daily or monthly budget; and stay with it. This means keeping your budget in mind, avoiding bidding wars if possible.

3. Bid just right.

Know how to bid right - a bid that is too high can exhaust all of your money, while a bid that is too low can make you lose that spot.

4. Watch the bottom line.

Measure your profit margin against your spending or expenses. Know when to stop and terminate your PPC program - if you spend more on advertising but have little or no sales at all.

5. Find the right keywords.

Decide which keyword phrases to opt and bid for. Do some keyword research, either by actually looking at existing search terms or with the use of online keyword suggestion tools, to know which terms are mostly used when searching for items that are related to your business. Focus on specific keywords, not on general ones.

6. Write effective ads.

A good PPC ad is that which can persuade and move a searcher. There are several approaches to this:

- Discount offers
- Testimonials
- Celebrity/famous endorsers
- Money-back guarantees
- Free trials or sample offers
- Freebies
- Reverse psychology
- Major benefits ("Teeth whitening")
- Direct instructions ("Click here")

7. Maintain a professional-looking site.

Your web content should be regularly updated and checked for spelling and grammatical errors. There should be no broken links or images. The website should be simple - designed in such a way that it will be easy for visitors to navigate and load. Include contact details to create a good impression among potential patients.

PPC – The Pros

- ✓ You need not be a genius in computer and technology to be able to run this ad campaign.
- ✓ Immediate results are seen after a few days.
- ✓ No need to make a website conform to the SEO rules.
- ✓ Nothing to lose even if you do not top the pages of different search engines. You can still always choose PPC advertising.
- ✓ You can make use any search engine available.
- ✓ You can type in any keyword you like.

PPC – The Cons

- ✓ Fixed payments every month to the search engine you choose.
- ✓ Pay for each click received by your website. At times, visitors are just competitors or people playing pranks on search engines. This hassle wastes money you put in to this advertising.
- ✓ Inability to pay for the fees next month would mean removal of your website on the paid listings.
- ✓ This advertising can only be used temporarily because it is difficult to handle in the long run.
- ✓ Pay-per-click pricing can be costly for long periods of time, therefore, this should be stopped after an ad campaign.

But how exactly PPC advertising can increase traffic, leads and new patient conversions?

PRE-QUALIFIED TRAFFIC. All visitors of your website are already considered as a qualified consumer or buyer of your services. PPC advertising leads your patients to you for a lesser cost.

www.ifusedentalmarketing.com

INSTANT EXPOSURE, IMMEDIATE PROFITS. PPC search engines enable you to get your desired results fast. They will have your website live within just a few hours which means immediate increase in sale.

CONSISTENT TOP LISTINGS. This is to get your website on top of the sponsored search results for free. You just have to choose the keywords related to your site and business and place them within your web pages. After this, you are done.

PPC advertising enables advertisers to control their advertising campaigns. Advertisers have effectively targeted their audience and set their own price per click. PPC advertising networks provide the platform to identify the desired audience by geographic setting, topic and industry. These networks have a list of websites of the publishers where the ads will be placed.

Tools are provided by the networks to check how the pay per click limit is working for a certain advertiser. If its still competitive, would it be even listed among the paid search lists or does it generate sales? Of course, if the advertiser made the highest bid, the better chances the ad will be seen in the search engine. These networks too provide protection for the advertisers against click fraud. This advertising set-up allows advertisers to set a daily budget for his ads, thus less spending for unnecessary clicks.

In PPC advertising, what are important are the keywords and phrases. You have to select at least 10 "very specific" keywords that would give you the best traffic in the search. Then, write the ad creatively but straightforward. Tell the truth about your product or service and do not lie. Good thing if your product or service will not disappoint those that are relying on your ad's promise - but what if it did otherwise? Important too is the clarity of the ad. Do not use very vague languages. Include important details like the price.

Important! You should also remember to budget your bids. Do not go overbidding because you will only lose your money and do not go so low that your ads will never get the chance to show up. Check your profit against your spending. If you see no progress then most likely you have to drop your ad campaign.

More and more dental practices have been using PPC advertising and it will continue to grow faster than any online advertising techniques. Search engines are making it harder and harder to optimize your website to rank organically, which will drive more advertisers to a pay per click platform.

PPC advertising is still relatively new in online marketing and it is going to continue in the years to come. For dentists, this means increased revenues with fewer advertising expenses, savings, more sales, good return of investment (ROI) and effective ad campaigns in the days to come.

How to Create a Profitable PPC Campaign

Certain keywords or phrases that people type into a search engine lead to hundreds and hundreds of search results that pertain to that specific keyword. Businesses that want to advertise on the net using a PPC campaign have to come up with a plethora of keywords that is associated to the business that they are running; so when potential patients type in these keywords, it will lead them to their business site.

This is pretty much the whole concept that operates behind PPC. This is how a PPC campaign brings in traffic to your site, with the selection of the right keywords that people can search through the net.

Some keywords tend to be more expensive than others, especially popular ones. It is vital to select the right keywords, in order to get your money's worth. This is why it is important to manage you PPC campaign wisely. Sometimes you are better off opting for the less popular keywords that are not so expensive, especially if you have a limited budget. Some businesses even hire the help of a consultant to manage their PPC campaigns.

There are a lot of experts that specialize in PPC campaign management. They come with strategic plans, and assess the need of their clients. They then come up with a PPC campaign that caters to their client's specification.

This is why big online businesses seek the expertise of a professional to run their PPC ad campaign, because the right set of plans, can potentially bring in a large amount of profits. The more keywords you have, the more you increase the chances of patients clicking these keywords that would lead them to your website. There are also some software you can purchase, such as Go Toast, or Bid Rank. These software programs track down your keywords listing.

Also, you should do some research before you start your PPC campaign. There are a lot of PPC search engines to choose from. Those who are less renowned charge less for the same keywords that you'd find in the bigger PPC search engines.

Most PPC search engines require a monthly payment in exchange for their services. But if you fail to make payments, they will automatically take your listings out of their search engines. So make sure that you pay your monthly bills, so all the efforts that you put into your PPC campaign don't go to waste.

PPC Bid Management

Search engines such as Google Adwords, Yahoo and Bing offer top positions among the sponsored listings for particular keywords/phrases you choose. The idea for bidding is you have to buy/bid on keywords/phrases relevant to your business. The highest bidder gets to be on the top of the search result listing and the second highest bidder, of course, gets the next top listing and so on. Every time a visitor clicks on your website, you will have to pay the same amount that you bid on that particular keyword.

PPC can be very costly, time consuming and sometimes not worthy. But if you know how to go about the step-by-step procedures, PPC is a welcome change to traditional advertising.

If you do your searches for products, articles and auctions in the net, you usually type in a keyword or a set of phrase to guide you in your search. Either you use Google or Yahoo Search depending on where you are most comfortable at and where you usually get the best results. As soon as you key in the search button, immediately a long list of keywords or phrase will be displayed containing the keywords you key in. The first or the top link that you saw is most likely the one who bids the highest for that keyword you type. In this way, businessmen will produce the desired results; they get to be advertised, at the same time, saving and spending only for the clicks they need that might translate to potential sales.

The way to start PPC bid management is to identify first the maximum cost per click (CPC) you are willing to pay for a given keyword or phrase. CPC varies from time and even search engine to search engine too. Maximum CPC can be measured by averaging the current costs of bids (bids range from $0.25 to $5). Average of these bids is to be used as the maximum CPC to begin with. As your ad campaign progresses, the actual conversion rate (visitors turning to potential buyers/sales) will be determined and you may have to adjust your CPC (bidding rate) accordingly.

When you start to bid, see to it that you adopt different bidding strategies for various search engines. Search engines have their own PPC systems that require different approaches. It is also worthy to identify different bids for the same keyword phrases in various search engines.

Another thing, it is wiser not to bid for the top spot for two reasons: 1) It is very expensive and impractical, and 2) Surfers usually try different search queries in various search engines before they settle on the right one that fits to what they are looking for. This hardly results to conversion. Try to bid for the fifth spot instead and work your way up.

If you are now going steady on your PPC biddings, it is time for you to develop your own bidding strategy accordingly. It is important for you to track down which sites bring the bulk of your traffic and identify the ranking of your paid ads. This will help your bidding strategy to be effective and you should also decide where you want your ad to be positioned. Usually your maximum CPC will limit your choices.

Bid gaps (e.g. $ 0.40, 0.39, bid gap, 0.20, 0.19, 0.18) occur when there is a significant price increase to move up one spot in the PPC rankings. It is best if you take advantage of the bid gaps by filling them in so you can save up your cents to other bidding opportunities. Often there are keywords worthy of lesser bids to get the appropriate ranking on the list and produce a good number of clicks and higher conversion rate rather than bidding higher but having a poor conversion rate. You have to put in mind that overbidding too is not good but rather the best position for the most effective bid.

Using pay-per-click bid management in promoting your website will only be successful if you take time building many lists across many engines and studying the performance of every listing. In this way, you can make the most value from what you spend in the bidding process. The key is to use the necessary precautions to stay ahead of the competition.

SEO or PPC?

The online community is definitely a large market place that you cannot ignore, especially if you have an Internet business. There are thousands if not millions of consumers that you can tap in the Internet.

At the same time, the Internet also poses a quite different challenge. The easy access that Internet provides also gives you as much competition as you can imagine. It is too crowded and congested.

Having a website is not enough to make your business running and able to compete. You must take other alternatives to give way for the online community to access your website at any rate or chance possible.

You have to expose your website. Make it known. It has to be visible. It has to be frequently targeted by consumers and surfers.

Invest in marketing your Internet site. There are basically two options available to you, the SEO and PPC. These two are probably the most desirable alternatives you can get for your Internet business as strategy for search engine marketing.

1. SEO

As we talked about in the last chapter, SEO stands for Search Engine Optimization. Some researches indicate that 60% - 70% of Internet surfers and users actually resort to using the Google search engine to find and locate web sites and pages, for any topic they desire. SEO is the process taken to make sure that the Internet uses will find your website when ranked among the top results of a search. This way you can make sure that you will be visible and can clearly stand out from the rest.

To get a search engine optimization, you will have to build on your own Internet site frequently hit Internet links to web site pages. The process will involve IBLN or Independent Back-Linking Network, wherein hundreds or even thousands of pages will be utilized to promote a particular website of a client.

In SEO, there is no need for you to pay for the clicks although it will require you to spend time doing research to get a favorable combination of ads and target audience. The SEO process is a long term one. It requires months, 6 months at the least, before the proper outcome is fully achieved, but once the goal is accomplished, you will definitely get a steady source of profit.

2. PPC

PPC gives way in advertising on a search engine. These are sponsored listings that you see whenever you make a search. There will be a charge whenever a visitor or web surfer clicks on any of your ads. There will first be a bidding process. The highest bidder for the price per click will definitely get the chance to be first listed in the search engine.

With this kind of advertising, you can still basically control your campaign as you get to create your own ad. You will also manage the target audience and still stay within the bounds of your budget. Most of the providers of PPC advertising will allow you to specify the target market, either by topic, industry or geographical location. You can also very well check if your ad gets to be shown at all and if it is competitive with the rest.

There are some guaranteed benefits when you get to maximize the PPC strategy.

PPC lets you advertise to the whole of the online community. It is also relatively easy to set up.

At first glance, PPC advertising may seem very expensive. Could it possibly happen that someone out there will go on clicking on your ad? This will definitely give you a large bill without the expected profit on your part. If this provides a lot of worries, be rest assured that there is a protection for you. Networks are able to recognize fraudulent clicks.

You can also set a budget for a certain period. The moment your budget has been used up by the target number of clicks, your ads will no longer be displayed until the next period you want it again displayed.

You will also be able to adjust well to changes in market demands and trends.

In deciding which of the two strategies will work right for you, think of your goals and of your resources. They definitely offer benefits and advantages that will work for your good. The better way to approach this two is to evaluate according to your short term and long term plans. Take the PPC course for your short-term goals and choose SEO if you have long term ones.

The world is out there for you now. Just make sure you do what will work best for your entrepreneurial endeavors and visions. The secret to success lies in your hands. Just study your options well and you'll get exactly what you want!

Strategy #7: Blogging

Blogging and social networking are inextricably linked in the sense that both contain certain features and certain properties of one another. Both are aimed at creating a wide movement as far as multimedia interaction is concerned. Though it is true that blogs can be regulated and kept very private, the main purpose of them is to reach out to a number of people, to have a medium to voice your opinion.

Another similarity is that both these concepts have existed in cyber space for almost a decade now, but in the initial stages both were rather exclusive of one another. Only in the recent times have they been merged, and their similarity in motives truly recognized.

Blogging is essentially done to channel your thoughts out on to an online journal. You also want other people to read what you have written. This way, you go about coming in touch with people from all over the world who you would not have otherwise known. Similar is the function of social networking. It is a hub where the young and the hearty flock. The chances of getting an audience at such a platform are high.

The origination of the term 'blog' is interesting. It was initially called a 'weblog' meaning a log or a diary or a journal that helps you to record your thoughts on a day-to-day basis. In that sense it was rather in its primitive stages and did not turn into an instrument for propaganda immediately. This term was later shortened to blog and this is when free blogging services like Blogger became extremely popular.

As mentioned earlier, blogging today is not restricted to only maintaining a journal. It has truly become a platform where various kinds of people from all walks of life, whether they have the same ideologies or not, conflate, and discuss the matters they think are important to them.

Blogging in the twenty first century has come to become an important tool for advertising for people who wish to market their products online, for politicians who wish to sell their ideologies, and reach out, to the masses.

Moreover, creating a blog and maintaining it does not require a fortune. Everybody now has a personal blog and it is all free of cost. Also, one does not need to be a computer engineer or a graphic or web designer in order to embellish their blog.

Unlike a website which operates on a different domain, and for which every single template and tab needs to be designed and created from the scratch, blog sites do not need such knowledge. The blogging service providers have their own inbuilt templates and fonts, which have to be chosen by the bloggers as per their own tastes and preferences.

Blogging is an ideal way to make new friends and come in contact with more people than you can do in the actual word, from all quarters of the world. Such diverse people will obviously have differing viewpoints. Therefore, this gives scope for a good deal of discussion and debate with all points of view being taken on board.

Blogs can also be for the sole purpose of making new friends and socializing. That is why social networking sites have picked up the clue and in these times social networking and blogging has, to some extent, been combined, and almost become indistinguishable.

It would be interesting to note that the word 'blog' is both a noun and a verb. This leads us to the fact that blogging in some sense also helps get rid of hassles of publishing. Though your work will not come out in print, you know that you can publish your work – your articles, pictures, videos, etc – yourself through you blog.

Therefore, it may be your own personal journal that you wish others to read or you works of art in terms of the stories or articles that you write, or the movies that you make. You can share almost any content with the world at large.

It must also be noted that just like you do not have to be a web designer to create your own blog, you need not be a professional writer, a filmmaker or a photographer to publish content on your blog. It is just a space for you to indulge in your own small artistic pursuits and share those moments with others. Blogging must therefore be exploited to its full potential.

How Can Online Blogging Be Profitable For Dentists?

Ranking of any website depends on a few factors. It would basically depend on the relevance of the article according to the key words used; the number of times that page has been linked and viewed, etc.

These are quite easy to follow, and if these factors are carefully noted and looked into, the rankings of your website can increase considerably.

The first step is to get your website linked through various other pages. The more the pages are that contain your links, the better ranking they will receive. The second aspect to be kept in mind is how often you update the content on your website.

Frequently edited and updated sites receive higher ranking in search engines than those that have not been looked at by the owners for ages. Always editing the content of your website as a whole may not be an option.

In this case what you can do is add a Blog to your website. A Blog will function as nothing but a forum for people to come and discuss the themes that concern your website too.

It will create a platform, as well as become a journal whereby you can also post updates about your operations and your website. The advantage is that the content on such Blogs will not be restricted only to text, but pictures and videos can be posted too.

The few easy steps as described below will take you through how to create your own blog and what are the things you must look out for:

Cost can never be a problem because free blogging services are quite popular all over the world. If you choose sites like Blogger or LiveJournal, you are sure to get exactly the kind of platform you are looking for. They are absolutely free.

If you are not very comfortable with web designing techniques, you need not worry. Creating your blog is not as complicated as designing template for a website. These blogging services provide a wide range of templates from which you can choose the one most suited to your tastes.

You must also use your discretion while blogging. Especially if you are incorporating your blog within your website, or creating a blog to increase awareness of your product, you need to keep in mind that this is an open forum which is read by all. You do not want to say anything that may end up angering your clients. Politics and religion are the two most controversial themes, and therefore anything about those must be carefully blogged about.

Anything that is particularly reader friendly and does not anger too many people is considered 'safe'. If your aim is indeed to increase the ranking of your site, you will have to make sure many people read it. You can do this by making your content user friendly.

Also keep an eye on what other people write or say on their blogs. This can give you a general idea of what kind of responses those articles receive, and you can get valuable tips from them.

Blogging has come to be considered a highly effective marketing tool.

You can easily create awareness of your product and get clients and patients to interact with each other. And not only patients, also those who are relatively new to your product get a platform to ask questions and clear their air about your product.

Moreover, it also increases your website rankings can increase because the blog is constantly being updates, commented on, and discussions are always going on. Because of its sheer activity, the rankings improve, creating more awareness of the product.

The following are the pointers based on which you can blog about your dental practice:

- Never make the blog post too long uselessly. It must be well written. Long posts tend to get dreary and they are not 'catchy' enough for people to sit and go through them.
- Update regularly. Since you don't need to write long posts, that is not much effort. Ideally, blog 3-7 times a week.
- Be entertaining where required, everyone can do with some lighthearted humor, without being derogatory.
- You need not stick only to text. Video and photo blogging are fast catching on and are interesting ways to share your thoughts, and make your videos and photographs well known.
- Be yourself. Do not imitate or copy someone else's content.

How to Start Your Own Blog in Less than 15 Minutes

Creating a blog is nothing that you need to be afraid of. There is no elaborate planning required either. However, there are a few things you would need to decide. Since these blogging service providers give you a lot of choice in terms of template and color themes, would be require to take those decisions yourself.

The following is a quick guide of what to think over before creating your blog:

Theme: Determine what you would be writing about or the nature of the content that you would be sharing with your readers. This depends mainly on your interest. Topics blogging to the field of politics, poetry, arts, current affairs, or almost anything under the sun can be chosen.

You can stick to one theme or you can choose to write about whatever concerns you on a day-to-day basis. Since it is your very own web journal, you can make it as flexible as possible in all aspects.

Blogging provider: Next you need to decide upon which blogging service provider you would like to use. This depends on the kind of reviews that you get about them from friends and acquaintances, or something about them that you may have read online. Otherwise, you can always try out something and find out if you like it. You can try out one of these popular sites: Blogger.com, WordPress.com, Typepad, Blogagotchi.com, Livejournal.com, JournalHome.com, TheDiary.org, Mindsay.com, Blog.com, Diaryland.com, Blogdrive.com, or Xanga.com.

Templates: A wide range of templates will be made available on any blogging service you decide to start you blog. Select the one you most prefer or like.

Freebies: The advantage with these blogging service providers is that they make your blogging experience as dynamic and interactive as possible. They enable you to install add-on features that include button, pictures, blog chalks, imoods, tagboards such as myshoutbox.com, guest maps, guestbooks, comment boxes for readers' thoughts and views, etc.

Additional features: These interesting ones may not be free. By paying a price you can avail of them.

Nature of blog: You must determine who should read your blog- whether you want it to be read only by a select circle, or must it be open to all. This will depend upon the content, mainly.

Layout: Again, there will be a wide range to choose from in terms of layout and color schemes.

Content: You could pick up a specific theme and write about it consistently, or merely decide on any random topic as and when it interests you. You could try putting up content for a while and see the kind of response you get, and alter or modify it accordingly.

Blogging circle: Blogging is a great way to come in touch with people from across the globe. You can surf and visit other people's blogs. Do not spam in their comment section, but write a genuine comment if you have something to say about a particular post.

Skins: You can customize and personalize your blog as much as you want. Using software like Photoshop you can create your own skins and make your blog attractive as well as make it reflect you own personality.

Publish: Finally when you are done selecting the setting and preferences, selecting a content to put up, you need to publish the content. Do not, however, forget to send the link to your blog to your friends and acquaintances so that they may come visit you.

Once you have started your blog, you will have noticed that it hardly takes fifteen minutes to do so. Maintain the blog is even easier. Here are a few tips that would help you successfully keep your blog going:

www.ifusedentalmarketing.com

Update: Update frequently otherwise visitors may stop coming to your blog. It will also give you more confidence to churn out more well worded posts in the future.

Personalize: Even though you might be discussing general and universal themes, add your own personal touch to make things lighter and interesting.

Theme: If you have a theme blog you can Google for other blogs of a similar kind and build you network.

Spelling and grammar: Make sure you proof read your posts. Spelling and grammatical errors can be a major put-off for many readers.

Advertisements: You could play host to sites like Google AdSense can earn revenue by placing their links on your blog.

Writing Content and Getting Constant Traffic to Your Blog

Blogging has truly revolutionized the way one experiences the digital age. There is, it seems, no limit to what one can do with the help of blogs. Even the smallest aspect of your daily personal life like recording journal entries has been given an entirely new dimension.

Going on from there, there is a lot of scope of picking up interesting debates and discussions through blogs. You can even start some of these discussions yourself. Moreover, there is nothing as interesting and attractive than that fact that you can even earn some money while blogging.

This is, by far, the most path breaking innovation that has entered the blog sphere. The requirements for this are very low. You need not be a scientist who posts revolutionary details about his latest experiment.

If you blog well, that is to say, if you blog well enough for people to come read it, you earn good chances of making quick money, by just going about your daily activity of posting blogs!

While writing your blogs you also need to keep in mind a few things. This is not only to ensure that you get a steady traffic, but also for the

fact that your blog readership can increase so that the ranking of your blog with search engines go higher. Here are a few tips that should see you through this:

Reader friendly content: At all costs keep your content – articles, poems, photographs, videos – reader friendly, that is to say, it should keep more and more readers interested. Your reader must be at the center of you post in a way that your reader must feel that he is gaining something out of reading your post. This is the basic rule in marketing.

Worthwhile: Never let the reader feel that he has been tricked into reading your post or clicking on your blog link. You are thwarting all your long-term chances of that reader coming back to your blog, in which case your blog rankings over the long term are in a dicey position.

Check for errors: Making grammatical and spelling errors can be a major put off for many readers. They may not visit your blog again simply because the errors that you make are too high. Always proof read your blog. A small typo here and there can be understood, but make sure you don't make any major errors.

KISS: Or, Keep It Short and Simple. This is the thumb rule you must follow at all point. Long winding posts tend to get boring. And it may contain nothing that is interesting to the reader. Also no one has the time enough for your blog, no matter how well you write. In fact, your blog will be much more appreciated if you put your thoughts simply and shortly.

Interesting: Make sure that you hold your reader's attention by making your posts snazzy. They must not be written in a tone that is tiring to read. Write short sentences and keep then crisp and precise. Always hit the point immediately in the course of your article.

www.ifusedentalmarketing.com

Link: Keep linking the blogs you read to yours in order to build a network those people will be in turn encouraged to link you. Remember, linking increases rankings.

Keywords: Using the keywords of your posts frequently increases the search ability of that particular article of yours which in turn leads more people to visit your blog.

Clear thoughts: Make sure you put your thought clearly before the readers so that it does not become tedious for them to read.

Colloquialism: You can write in a friendly tone. Avoid using too many slang words, but otherwise, if your post demands it, you can be colloquial.

Post title: A catchy post title or headline is half your business solved. It can glue a reader to your post almost immediately. However, do not put misleading post titles, or you will lose creditability.

So, be consistent with your blog content and watch traffic flowing in to your blog!

There are a lot more brilliant ideas for generating a high quality lead list. But the most important thing to consider is that you should lead people to your personalized local business lead capture process, so your leads can be high quality and directly interested in your own services.

Chapter V

Highly Effective Local Marketing Tips

Tip #1: Provide an online free service: Providing a free service on the web is a great way to create brand awareness in your local community. Every time they see your brand somewhere on the street they will remember you and might stop by your business place.

They will even be more aware of your offers and special occasions just to check out what hot promotion you are having at the moment. Besides grabbing their attention, they will constantly be remembering you every time they use that product or service you gave them for free.

A good example of this is when you can offer a "free cleaning" or "free teeth whitening" when combined with a new patient visit.

Tip #2: Show your local personality over the web: It is very important to show your unique personality to your local audiences on the web. That will make them exited once they know you in person, it will give them trust.

You can use places like your local business website, your local business social media accounts. You can even create Videos about your practice, showing your local office as well as your staff.

Tip #3: Stay on brand: Avoid promoting other brands. If you need to show other brands make sure it's only for the purpose of letting them know what services you actually offer in your local office.

If your services are unique, there is no point in promoting what tools, services or training material you use in creating your services. Promote only your brand everywhere.

Tip #4: Capture leads: As you may know by now, there are so many ways to capture leads for your practice. Capture as many leads as possible by using as many lead generation techniques as possible.

But remember to focus on the techniques that allow you to get high quality leads. Don't be deceived by those crazy online services offering you thousands and millions of leads for $20 or $40 bucks. Those are not Quality Leads at all.

Tip #5: Digital banner ads work locally: The Google+ display network allows local businesses to create banner ads and display them in community websites. These ads will not be displayed outside of a specific area.

With Google AdWords PPC ads and Facebook ads you can target your local audience as well. It is less cost efficient but it can send great message to your audience.

Tip #6: Think like the patients: Walking a little in your patient's shoes will be one of the greatest things you will ever do for the success of your practice. You must be a patient in order to really understand your practice.

Think what online tools you can create that may help your patients enjoy a lot more of your services: training, a complete updated blog, online support, even online purchases, which will be just amazing for them too.

Tip #7: Be different and creative: People like new stuff, it's true that a set pattern that has been proven to work will keep working, and that's a really strong fact online too, but being unique will also bring its own great benefits.

Of course don't leave that proven pattern, but just try to add your personal touch to it, and also adapt it to your local patients. A promotion in California may not work as well in Virginia, so be aware of that too.

Tip #8: Build links and social signals: When you build links to your website, remember natural links are the best kind of link. You can create a blog on your website and update it constantly.

You can provide useful information to your audience and they will spread it for you. When your audiences share your information on Facebook and other social media, your information creates strong social signals and search engine love.

Tip #9: Get personal: You can send personalized emails and messages to your potential and valued patients. You can post fun questions in the social networks which will make your followers talk about it - people love to respond.

The Majority of patients respond to personalized content rather than non-personalized content. You should create relevant content that your audience is looking for and give them more of what they care about and less of what they don't care about.

Tip #10: Create a mobile app: I can tell you this: every important practice has created a mobile app that does something very useful for their potential patients.

A practice could use their app to allow instant scheduling. You could offer appointment reminders through the app or you could even promote specials, coupons and recent patient reviews on it.

The possibilities of a Mobile App are endless.

Chapter 6

Shocking Local Marketing Case Studies

These are not all dental marketing case studies, but it will give you some good ideas on how other industries are using local marketing to jump-start their businesses.

Case Study #1: Hue & Cry

Hue and cry Inc. is a family company; it sells security and life safety products and services in Northern California and Southern Oregon. They needed more traffic to their website to generate more sales leads to support their business mission.

After analyzing the competitive landscape, they published a blog and posted original content on that blog twice in a week. The Blog was optimized for organic search engine rankings. Top search engine rankings and high quality content brought more website traffic. Their website traffic increased 31% and their blog accounts got more than half of all the website traffic.

Case Study #2: Georgia Roofs

Georgia Roofing & Repair, Inc. is a local Atlanta Residential & Commercial Roofing & Interior Construction Company. The Company was facing some troubles and wanted a new way to reach their patients.

They used Search Engine Optimization and Search Engine Marketing to target their prospects in the client's area.

They also implemented a contact and tracking system to convert their online traffic into paying patients.

As result they got 200 new leads in the first month and their average conversion rate was 50%. They doubled their business productivity within the first month.

Case Study #3: On Time Air Conditioning & Heating, Inc.

On Time Air Conditioning & Heating, Inc. is a local HVAC company. Kristi started this business so that she could take care of patients and their comfort.

www.ifusedentalmarketing.com

The company decided to use local marketing on the web to increase their overall leads, new patients and sales by leveraging the number of online searchers looking for their products and services.

They used Local SEO, Local PPC (Google AdWords), and Marketing Consulting services for their company. As a result, the Company was able to increase their ROI by 454% in the first 2 ½ months of their online marketing activities.

Case Study #4: Platinum Realty Network

Platinum Realty Network is a full service Concierge Style Real Estate Brokerage licensed in Arizona. It focuses on making real estate transactions painless and stress-free for clients.

The Company decided to use Local Marketing on the web to increase traffic and generate leads.

They wanted to improve their PPC Advertising. Their PPC campaigns were not performing as they originally had hoped. The leads coming through these campaigns were very expensive.

The Company used Local PPC, List Building and Marketing Consulting to improve their traffic and drive down their cost per lead.

This Real Estate Firm increased their Overall Lead Generation by 79% with a Targeted PPC Campaign in a Market that Some Were Calling 'Dead'.

Case Study #5: Lights for less

This Company worked for several local home and furniture companies. After some years they ramped up an online marketing solution for 'Lights for Less' – a discount lighting store.

They launched a brand new domain name and website, optimized it for the search engines and provided an ongoing strategy for online marketing with a limited budget.

They're a local retail shop in a small town in Ohio. They continued to make themselves visible to potential patients in Brunswick and surrounding areas.

Their direct traffic increased 15.89%, their search engine ranking increased 72.90%, and page views increased 141.44%.

Case Study #6: Black McCuskey Souers & Arbaugh

Black McCuskey has served their clients, the community and the legal profession as one of the leading law firms in the State of Ohio.

They wanted to increase their local traffic from search engines. They used extensive keyword research within all of their priority practice areas and then used the results of that information to optimize their CMS system.

Black McCuskey's website traffic increased 50% after one year with a simple investment in research and optimization.

Case Study #7: Richter Orthodontics

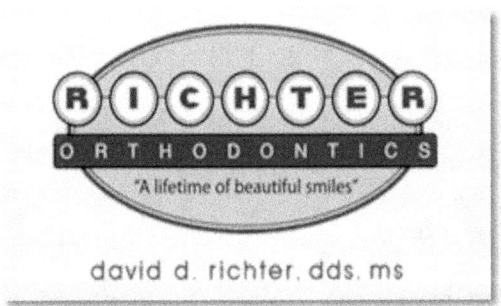

Dr. David Richter wanted to launch his website and his goal was to draw in new patients by expanding his brand awareness in the Greeley community as well as the surrounding rural areas.

Richter Orthodontics needed to optimize their local listing to distinguish themselves from the crowd in their marketing niche. They optimized their website with unique title tags, Keyword Analysis and Meta descriptions to help out their potential patients. They also ran a strong link building campaign by submitting the domain to industry specific directories.

In just one month, new visitor traffic increased 12.91%, PPC Ads Attracted 221 Clicks & over 21,500 Impressions.

Case Study #8: Legends Training Centre

Legends Training Center has been operating a state-of-the-art facility that offers fitness programs including Gracie Barra Jiu Jitsu, Boxing, Kickboxing, Grappling, and Mixed Martial Arts. The problem was that their old traditional advertising campaigns were expensive and not delivering good results.

They used integrated online marketing strategies with search engine optimization, online advertising and campaigns for their local business and saw instant results.

Student enrollment grew with an "attract, convert and retain" online marketing automation strategy. This boosted the website's exposure, and visits increased 835% in two months.

Case Study #9: Koala Outdoor Services

Koala Outdoor Services is a local company that provides commercial and residential landscaping services including maintenance free decks, fencing, grading, retaining walls, patios, and full landscape design services.

The Owner Amir Mazor wanted to grow his business but he wasn't an expert in marketing and the return he was getting for his marketing efforts was too small.

He knew that he delivered the most value to his business when he was on-site delivering projects for his patients, so he wanted to focus on an online marketing strategy for his local business.

They created a website optimized with SEO to attract new visitors and used lead nurturing and campaign tracking to handle their website with an online survey.

The survey collected testimonials from happy patients. And the website visitor traffic increased by 136% within three months and requests for fencing, decks and landscape work are now turning into leads on a daily basis.

Case Study #10: Sandlapper Soaps

Sandlapper Soaps, a primarily online retailer, was looking for suggestions for the best way to positively impact their bottom line. They used Website Design and Usability Consulting - SEO Audit, SEO / Search Optimization and Social Media to increase their local traffic.

And the result was surprising, On-site sales conversion rate increased 33.52% and Natural SEO traffic increased 300%. Stronger calls-to-action to join Sandlapper's community increased its mailing list numbers by 50%. It allowed retailers to increased profit margins by 12%

Chapter 7

Dental Marketing Dos and Don'ts

Do's:

Optimize your website for mobile: Make it easy for patients and followers who use mobile devices, tablets and Smartphones. Smartphone and tablet users use their mobile devices two to six times in a week to search local businesses.

Assure accurate information: You should keep your information accurate and constantly updated and accessible throughout the web and on all publisher's listings. These will increase your search engine ranking.

Offer high quality content: Your website content should be impressive and useful for your patients. It will make it easy for your patients to leave reviews about your business. Quality and effective reviews leave a good impression on your patients, it also influences your search engine ranking.

Update your profile: You should update your business profile from time to time with updated images, new product or new services. Search engines love consistency. Your patients will want to know more about your new products and services.

Include media: Videos and Images increase your appeal in your local market by making your offerings more tangible. Search engines love them. Visuals can boost your business rankings and appeal in the market.

You can include patients' testimonials, product demonstrations and customer service staff in your videos and images to make it more powerful.

Correctly optimize the on page signals: On page SEO is associated with page title, URL, header tags, image alt text, and page content. You can consider the geographic area in which you provide service, including suburbs or nearby towns.

You can place keywords, language and content to describe your business and the area with a consistent NAP (name, address and Phone) listing on online directories. This will help local searchers find your business.

Stand out: You should always try to be different and creative to stand out from the crowd in your marketing niche. You should tell your audience what you are providing that your competitors don't. You can give them a reason to purchase from you.

Utilize social ambassadors: Social media pages work as a brand ambassador. Some people check their Facebook account more often than their mailbox. You can create mini pages to drive your traffic to your business blog and utilize the social platforms to get more traffic.

Use a strong call to action: You can include a call to action on your business website. You can run an offer, free coupons, % off on services, etc. People always look for offers. With this you can get a great deal of traffic to your website. You can also include this offer information on your landing page.

Claim your profile: You can list your business in local directories. Each directory serves different purposes, but overall they increase your visibility on the web.

You can claim your business on Google Places, Yelp, Manta, Bing Business Portal and others. Power Listings allow you to claim your local business in more than 30+ local search sites in a few minutes.

Don'ts:

Don't create fake reviews: Do not write fake reviews for your practice. Search engines are getting better at detecting fake reviews, so be able to stay away from that. If you post fake reviews you might face a penalty that can harm your practices' local search engine ranking for a long time.

Don't spam your patients: Just because you have the customer's contact information that does not mean you should go crazy with your marketing strategies and send them an email every hour. If you do this, your patients will definitely unsubscribe from your lead list forever.

Don't set it and forget it: Remember things change on the web, you've gotta keep an eye on all the online services you are using for your local marketing. Social Media as well as various online marketing tools are updated often. You must be aware of that for your local online marketing efforts too.

Don't use a P.O. Box address: If you use a P.O. Box address for your practice then it will be difficult for the search engine to determine where your practice is located geographically. You should always use your physical address as your business address.

Don't focus only on new patients: You should appeal to both new and existing patients. New patients are quite interested in your contact information and support unlike existing patients who are often interested more in your products, discounts and new offers.

Don't rely only on search engine traffic: Local people don't always use Google, Bing, Yahoo or other directories to find businesses around their local area. A significant number of local searchers use review sites, portals, applications and other tools to find you.

Don't over optimize: Search Engine Optimization is important, but do not try to over optimize your website. Search engines penalize those who try to game the ranking code to get in the top no matter what. Try to optimize for several keywords at the same time instead of just one.

Don't use a toll-free number: Using a toll-free telephone number will make it very difficult for the search engines to find your geographical location. Using a land-line phone number will help you avoid this. Besides that, a land-line number will make you look more professional and real.

Don't ignore negative Reviews: Negative reviews are a great opportunity to make your product or service even better each time until its perfect. Be kind to people who offer Negative Reviews, thank them for being honest. And tell them you actually use negative feedback to make your product a lot better.

Don't pay to be in directories: You don't have to pay to be in local directories. They don't provide any extra facility to your business. These types of directories are spammy and search engine don't like them.

Chapter 8

Video Marketing

Prior to television, commercials used to be aired on the radio. Before radio, businesses used to advertise their wares in a variety of different ways, mostly through print media. Even before print media, metal signs depicting the nature of the product were produced. For as long as there have been people in business, they have sought different ways to advertise their business. The purpose was to get more sales leads and generate more revenue for the business. Things have not changed. Although advertising has come a long way, the nature of the reason for advertising has not changed since the days of the metal signs.

Radio commercials used to often feature jingles. The purpose of these jingles were to make the listener remember the product. Remember that people could not visualize the product back then, so they identified with the jingle. Commercial jingles were so popular, they were also later used in television advertising, although they seem to have lost their appeal.

Early radio advertisers were the sponsors of the radio program. They were short and sweet and people were forced to listen because they didn't want to miss the next installment of their favorite radio show. Plus, back in those days, there was no remote control.

When television came out in the late 1940s, advertisers quickly saw this as a good media to sell their product. They began sponsoring certain television shows. They often found ways to not only sponsor by their frequent commercials, but also within the program itself. One example of this is the old "I Love Lucy" television program, probably one of the most popular sitcoms of all times. It was sponsored by Phillip Morris. Lucille Ball and Desi Arnaz had stipulations in their contract that they had to often be seen smoking during the program. This is why Ricky was often seen coming out of his child's bedroom with a cigarette hanging out of his mouth.

In return for their sponsorship, the program aired. People were treated to all sorts of commercials in black and white that would seem very amateurish to people today. Madison Avenue was always the place for the big "ad men." It soon became apparent that in addition to designing clever ads for magazines and billboards, they had to film commercial ads. The needed actors and cameras, lights and sets. Was it worth it?

There were those businesses who thought that television would never last. They balked at the idea of spending a lot more money to advertise on television. And they certainly didn't want to pay to sponsor an entire program. Most of those businesses have now gone out of business.

Television advertising is a multi-billion dollar business. Commercial jingles from the past are still remembered fondly but advertisers have become more creative and many big businesses have decided to put a lot more money into their advertising. A good example of this is the Super Bowl. The ads that are broadcast during this annual football event are the most expensive ads in the business. Companies spend millions of dollars not only creating the clever ad that they hope will "stand out among the others" but also for the time they need to pay to have their commercial aired. Things have changed since "I Love Lucy." No longer are the programs grateful to the sponsors, now the sponsors are grateful to the programs. There are many people who watch the Super Bowl every year just to see the new and very clever ads. And the next day at work, the ads are more discussed than the actual game.

People are visual. And advertising is effective. As more people began using the Internet, advertisers turned to this new media to promote their sales. They used print ads and pop up ads most of the time. Then they began to realize that what worked for television may also work for the Internet. According to UCLA studies, 82 percent of the people in the United States use the Internet. And many use it much more than they watch television. Advertisers took the next logical step and began promoting video advertising on the Internet. At first, it began small. Print ads that could be clicked on. Then they moved to more clever banner ads with animation. Now they are moving to video advertising.

You have probably seen video advertising on the Internet, many of the news websites use this. According to a study done by the Chicago Tribune Online, more people click on to the videos than read the news articles. Video advertising is here to stay. And it is now up to dentists to use this new media to make begin increasing their patient base through video advertising on the Internet.

Here you will learn just who uses video advertising, how it is used, where it is used and the many different ways it can be used to promote your practice. Do you want more patients? More profits? Unlike television advertising, video advertising on the Internet does not have to cost a lot of money. It can be simple or elaborate, but either way, it is much more effective than a print ad.

This chapter will tell you how you can increase your sales profits by video advertising. It will tell you the different ways video advertising can work. It will explain the difference in costs and the limitless possibilities that this technology can increase your practice's sales and profits.

Those practices who shun new often regret it. There has never been a better time to learn about how to promote your practice through video advertising and increase your sales. You do not have to be a technical expert. You do not have to have a lot of money. You do not have to hire actors. You simply have to present your practice to your target audience in a way that will make them want to buy your product. Come with us into the future and learn more about video advertising.

People Are Visual

Sad but true, most people would rather watch television than read a book. People love to be entertained. Ever since the advent of television, people began staying inside and watching TV rather than going out with friends. Television has more of an influence on society during the 20th century than anything else. Until the Internet. Then things started to change. In addition to just watching television, people could find out information, interact with others and even make money on auctions. And each year, the Internet becomes more sophisticated. There are billions of websites out there in Internet land. People are now spending more time on the Internet than they are watching television. And now that most of the country is on the Internet, they are also finding different ways to be entertained online.

In the early days of the Internet, most of the information was written. You looked up information and read it. If there was a photo, it caught your eye. People soon began using clip art and other visual effects in their ads, e-mails and websites. It was soon discovered that websites and advertisers who used some form of visual stimulation were attracting more people to their site. This included everyone. Internet communities, such as MySpace began popping up for people to meet and network. These included easy ways that one could download a photo of themselves or friends. It also included ways they could design their pages to make them more attractive.

Which would you rather look at? An attractive, well designed page or a typed written article written in black font on a white background. Of course you would rather look at the attractive page. You are not alone. Human beings are highly visual. Even a cartoon photo can be a source of entertainment and can get someone to read what you want them to read. Have you ever received an e-mail that featured photos or a cartoon? Wasn't that more entertaining than one that featured a text joke (that you already heard 100 times before)?

THE ULTIMATE GUIDE TO INTERNET MARKETING FOR DENTISTS

In the early days of the Internet, advertising consisted of either printed ads that were put on different websites to attract patients and ad banners. When people clicked on to the banner, the owner of the website got money. This was the way the advertisers kept track of which websites were worth their advertising dollars. These advertising vehicles are still being used, but are quickly becoming a thing of the past.

Then pop up ads became popular. People would be on a website and an ad would pop up suddenly. Sometimes it looked like it was part of the site. It would take you to another website for advertising. Sometimes, it was just gathering your information so that you could be barraged by constant e-mails.

The pop up ads were ineffective. Although they attempted, like all ads, to reach a target audience, many people found them annoying. Soon there was a way to block pop up ads from appearing. Many people now use this tool as an option on the Internet.

News media soon found that it was very effective to put not only the news coverage of an important case, but actual video clippings. They soon discovered that more people were watching the videos than reading the news. It was easier to do and, more importantly, entertaining. News websites were among the first to realize the impact of adding video to their websites. Now many other companies are following suit.

American people want to be entertained. They want to be entertained on television, at the movies and on the Internet. And they even expect their advertisements to be entertaining. A simple banner advertisement has no chance against a good video advertisement. Particularly if it is both informative and has a bit of humor. Not only will the person watch the video, they will share it with others. They will place it on their own websites and blogs and even e-mail it to friends.

www.ifusedentalmarketing.com

Entertainment is the key to good advertising. Gone are the days of the catchy commercial jingle. The banners will soon be on their way out, too. The dental advertisers who are truly adding to their business are using video advertising in many different ways to draw patients to their products. And the more patients they attract, the more business they get and the more profit they make.

If you truly want to move into the new age of advertising, now is the time. Not only is video advertising on the Internet cheaper than commercial advertising, it can be done by just about anyone. You do not have to be Francis Ford Coppola to make a video. Sometimes, the most quirky and funny videos are those that are remembered the most.

If you have a website, (and I hope that you do!) it is just as easy to add video as it is to add photographs and texts. Of course you will still have the text and photos, but people will be more intrigued by the video. Particularly if it is entertaining and grabs their attention.

Suppose, for example, you want to sell your home. You want to list it on the Internet with a price. But you do not include a photo of the home. Chances are, your home listing will not be viewed nearly as much as those with photos.

Suppose you want to advertise for a date on an Internet dating site (please don't do this!). But you do not want to add your photo. Chances are that no one will read your profile and think about what a wonderful person you are even if you are Prince William. They will see you have no photo and go on to the next.

Why is this? Because people are visual. They need visual stimulation. They need to imagine themselves in the home or on a date with you before they will even think of contacting you. And do not kid yourself, Internet dating is also a form of advertising. And those with photos get much more attention than those without.

Now suppose you want to sell your home and you decide to do something different. Instead of posting a photo of your home on the website, you take a video of the home. You move from room to room with the camera and describe the details. It will make people feel as though they are inside the home. And, virtually, they are. How well do you think that advertisement will do against the home ads with no photos or even those with photos? I guarantee it will do a lot better. You may even be able to ask a higher price.

People do not often have the imaginations we would like to give them credit for. For years they have received their news information, weather reports, sports games and entertainment from television. This has been going on for the past 50 years. And as the entertainment industry has grown, the audience has grown more demanding. They want more visuals. No more implications. No more "leave it to the imagination." They want to see every detail on the screen.

What makes you think that Internet advertisement is any different? Do you honestly think that you are going to get more traffic with a small banner ad or an e-mail with a bunch of long paragraphs than a video ad?

Think about having an exciting new dental procedure for a special type of patient. You want to tell your patient all about it, but it is complicated. It may be technical and too difficult for the patient to comprehend. At best, they will skim over the article. At worst, they will not even read it.

What if, instead, you sent them a video of the procedure in operation? Do you think they will be more or less interested? If you are unsure about the answer, as yourself the same question. What would you rather see? A video demonstration of an exciting new procedure or a two page e-mail telling you about it? You know the answer. It is the same reason that you would rather watch the football game on television than listen to it on the radio. Because you, like all human beings, are visual.

Now you need to learn how to make that knowledge work for you by using video advertising on the Internet to advertise your business.

Who Uses Web Videos To Promote Business?

After reading a little about web videos for advertising, you may be asking yourself just what type of businesses are taking advantages of this media? The answers are just about everyone who understands the concept of entertainment in advertising.

Just about every business that has a website on the Internet is now adding some sort of video advertising to their sites. This ranges from car dealerships, travel agents, real estate agents and even manufacturers. They realize that they get the attention of a viewer right away if a video comes onto the screen instead of a simple advertisement.

Department stores are also beginning to use video advertising on the Internet not only on their websites, but also on Internet advertising engines such as Google. It simple captures the attention of a potential buyer more than just a plain photo.

Imagine that you have a website that sells T-shirts, for example. A person goes to your website and sees a variety of T-shirts that are for sale. These are often pictured in photos either by themselves or on models. The prices are included, along with an ordering form. Most websites have a search option so if someone is looking for a particular T-shirt, they can find it easier.

The reason models are depicted in T-shirts is to make the product more attractive. More people are apt to purchase a garment featured on a striking model than an average person or on a mannequin. This is simply another way people are visual. They imagine themselves as the model in the T-shirt and feel that they will also look this way once the garment is acquired.

Now imagine you have this same website but decide to implement video advertising as part of your campaign. Instead of clicking on to a website that just depicts a bunch of models in T-shirts, you have a video where a model is wearing the T-shirt and talking about how much she loves her T-shirts from your company.

Or, you decide to go the humor route. A video depicts an unpopular, geeky kid wearing a white shirt with a pencil protector in the pocket and getting his books knocked out of his hands at school. He says something like "I've had enough of this, I'm getting myself over to XXX T-shirt company!"

The next clip shows the same student wearing one of the T-shirts and surrounded by a bevy of women. He winks at the camera and says, "XXX T-shirt changed my life - they can change yours, too."

Corny? Yes. But entertaining and memorable. As a matter of fact, the more humor or unusual aspects you can add to your video, the more people will remember it. They may even like it so much that they post it on their blog or on "You Tube." Then you get even more advertising for your business. For free.

Travel agents are quickly discovering that video is the way to go when it comes to advertising on the Internet. More and more travel agencies are not just depicting photos of exotic places, but videos of the attractions that can be seen when visiting these places. People feel as though they are taking a trip. They sometimes call this a "virtual tour" and it is really quite effective. A virtual tour takes the viewer on a mini vacation all from their home computer. They get to see highlights of the wonderful sights, the hotels, the beaches and a lot of people enjoying themselves. This sparks their imagination. They envision themselves on the tour and it makes them want to visit as well. The more someone knows about the positive aspects of a particular tour, country or vacation spot, the more apt they are to want to book a vacation to this destination.

Speaking of virtual tours, we have already talked about real estate agents in the last chapter. Many real estate companies are now adding video advertising to their websites. Instead of just seeing photos of a home, they see the entire home, just as they were touring it.

In addition to large businesses and professionals using video advertising on the Internet, musicians are learning the value of this technology to promote their music and bands. Music videos came out in the 1980s and were frequently depicted on MTV. This was a very popular concept, but soon became very competitive. More and more money was being used to make a more 'creative video" for the band. Bands who had creative videos depicting models or something unusual were selling more music than other bands who did not have the capital to create such videos.

In the 1980s, video cameras cost over $1,000. And if you wanted the video to look professional, you had to hire a director and some actors. The music videos of the 1980s were actual commercials for a particular artist or a band. And they cost a lot of money to produce.

Today, not only professional musicians advertise by video on the Internet, but amateurs as well. Video cameras no longer cost over $1,000. They are easy to use and the content can easily be downloaded into a personal computer. It is just as easy to upload a video into your webpage as it is to upload a photograph or music. So amateur musicians began promoting their bands on the Internet. On MySpace, for example, there are thousands of artists doing this. They do not even have to pay for their MySpace page. It is free. They simply have to have someone film their act with a camcorder, upload it to their site and they are advertising for free on the Internet. It sure beats the old days of recording demos for thousands of dollars and trying to find someone on the radio to play them.

Individuals who have something unique to sell are also using video advertising on the Internet. They can do this with little or no expense if they choose a venue like You Tube. You Tube allows anyone who is a member to upload their videos for others to see. The more clever the video, the better chance of it being discovered. If you want to draw people to your website, mention it in your funny video and put it on YouTube. Millions of people use this website every day. The videos are often either e-mailed to friends or put on blogs and other spaces. Suppose you have invented a special item to sell. You have a patent but have no idea how to sell it. You have a website and are trying to promote it, but are not having much luck. You can advertise on television, but it costs a fortune; even on cable TV.

Maybe you can come up with a funny video that will draw people to your website that involves your product. You can post this on your site and then wait for people to discover the ad. You can also place it on such video websites as YouTube.

Car dealerships are another business that are using video technology to advertise on the Internet. Car dealerships have always been known for their "over the top" approach to advertising. They sometimes run specials depicting happy patients getting great deals, or they show a video of a car being driven down the road and being able to make great turns. This cost them much less than advertising on television.

So, how do you think a dental practice could use video marketing and ads? At our agency, we offer a wide variety of video placements. These include interviews with the dentist in a live interview fashion, think CNN, we also have our video crews go into the office and shoot the staff, docs in action, lobby, and even interview patients. There are a wide variety of ways to use video for your dental practice.

Is Video Advertising Expensive?

If you are already advertising on the Internet, you know the costs of having banners or pop up ads. Video advertising is not much more money and is twice as effective. If you do not believe this, check it out. You can try this for a month and see if you get more stats on the video ads or the banner ads. Most advertising engines agree that their patients profit get many more views on their video advertising than plain text or even photo advertising.

Cost will depend on how you wish to use the video to market your practice. If, for example, you simply want to use a video on your website, it will not cost anything. Just the uploading of the video into the website. If you want a more professional looking video for your website, there are plenty of companies out there that provide this service for much less than text advertising. You can have a slick ad or you can have one that is home made. Sometimes, the homemade videos tend to stand out more.

It will cost you slightly more to have your videos featured on other websites where you advertise. More than a banner ad or a line ad. But again, how much is your practice worth to you? If you want to see how effective this media is, test it out.

If you want to advertise for free, there are plenty of places on the Internet where you can post your videos. They will also give you stats on how many people have viewed your video. On some websites, the videos are rated.

There are many professional companies that can help you out with video advertising. They can offer everything from creating the video, uploading onto the proper websites to even using it in e-mails to your patients. Many practices keep a database of their clients. If they don't, they should. From time to time, they have wish to contact their patients by e-mail. E-mail is very inexpensive. Actually, it is free. You can either hire a professional to e-mail your patients your advertising video or do it yourself to save even more money.

Writers are gaining publicity for themselves by using videos on writing websites. They upload a video of themselves and talk about their work. This is an excellent way to get people to read your work, particularly if you are on a site that pays you for page views. You can do this in an interview format, or simply have someone film you talking about yourself. This is free.

You can also promote yourself or your practice on YouTube for free. Camcorders have come down significantly in price. Many are around

$100 or even cheaper. Each year, the price goes down and the quality goes up. They are easy to use and the contents can be uploaded to your computer with ease. Then all you have to do is decide where you want to "advertise."

How many of you get e-mails from businesses that you have previously done business? Most of you do, I would suspect. Even if you clicked on their ad by some mistake, they will contact you via e-mail. As said previously in this chapter, e-mail is free.

Now, imagine that you get an advertisement from a business that has a very funny video attached to it? You will be entertained and not forget about that business. It may even prompt you to take a look at their sale or new promotion.

I saw one of the most effective and clever uses of advertising on the web recently. I was taking a look at shower filters. Instead of just a website, like most of them, that featured shower filters and explained the advantages of having one of these gadgets, this one had a scene from the movie "Psycho." Yes, the shower scene. The caption was "Remember when the only thing you had to fear about the shower was…." and then it stopped. We saw the familiar scene of Janet Leigh in the shower and "Mother" coming through the door with the knife. It was clever, entertaining and certainly caught my attention. In fact, this was the company that I decided to purchase the shower filter from.

www.ifusedentalmarketing.com

How much did this ad cost them? A little more than a regular video ad. The film "Psycho" is not in the public domain so they had to pay synchronization rights to the producer to use this on their website. But synchronization rights on film, even the Internet, are based upon seconds. They did not have to pay for the rights for the entire film, just a brief portion of the shower scene.

If you have a clever imagination, you can film your own video that will attract attention to your project in the way that this shower filter company did. You can purchase synchronization rights from film producers if you want, or you can simply make up your own video. Also, be aware that many films made prior to 1962 lie within the public domain. This means that they are free to use. Clips can be obtained from all over the Internet, or can be downloaded from your television or DVD player. You must make sure that the film is in the public domain, however. The way to do this is to check with the United States Copyright Office. There is also much information about which films lie within the public domain on the Internet.

No, it is not expensive to advertise using video on the Internet, particularly if you are advertising on your own website or e-mailing your patients video advertisements. Just make sure that the advertisements are not too long or it may bore the customer, no matter how entertaining it may be. You do not want to go more than 30 seconds to 3 minutes.

If you decide to use an Internet advertising agency, they can keep track of the amount of patients who view your video and make sure that they are placed in the proper venues.

The cost is not that much more than banner ads and may be well worth it. Banner ads are sometimes clicked on by accident, giving false stats. A video ad, however, can be managed where the person has to click on to the "play" button to view it. Once they begin viewing, chances are that they will continue to do so. Either way, at least you will have an honest count of viewers when it comes time to pay Google or whoever you are using for your Internet advertising. In a way, the difference in the quality of the views more than makes up for the price difference in advertising.

What About Video Promotion?

Perhaps, by now, you have already decided to join the 21st century and become part of the video advertising on the Internet world. Just like many other smart business people and other individuals.

You have now realized that video advertising is not only more effective, but may end up costing you less money in advertising in the long run. We have also talked about different ways you can do your own marketing using video advertising for free.

If you have decided to contact an advertising company about using video advertising on the Internet, such as Google or Yahoo, which is now coming out with a new program, you will have many different options as to where your videos can be placed.

Just like television advertising, you will want to reach your target audience. This means that a video advertising a rock band will not be promoted on a website that deals with travel. The wonderful thing about using a professional service is that they know exactly what websites are out there and where to promote your video.

Costs for using a professional advertising agency will depend upon how often you want the video used, the sites you want it to be used on, and the length of the video. Naturally, if you want your video splashed across Yahoo's front page, it is going to cost you a lot more than if you want it on a blog that accepts Google ads.

Perhaps you are offering a three day stay in Disney World as a new patient special (I know this is crazy). You will want your target audience to be people with children. There are many different family oriented websites on the Internet, parenting advice websites and so forth. The advertiser will know where to find them and how much it will cost to advertise. This is what you are paying for - their expertise of knowing the best websites on which to advertise on the Internet.

If you do not want to spend a lot of money but have a quirky type of ad that can generate new patients and maybe has a little humor to it, it may be advertised on someone's blog. Many people have discovered the joy of blogging and certain Internet blogging websites offer Google ads for bloggers. The ads are free and the person who blogs gets a little bit of money every time someone clicks on your ad. The advertisers know the blogs that get the most traffic and your quirky little ad might just start making the rounds all over the Internet.

If you want to place the video ad on your website or on free Internet websites that allow videos, you will have to make sure that your contract stipulates that you have the right to do this. While some advertising companies will allow you to promote your own ad, others will not. Some want exclusive rights. If the advertising company actually developed the video ad for you, they will retain exclusive rights and you will not be able to use it anywhere without their written permission.

Video ads can go just about anywhere banner ads go. The beauty of the video ad, however, is that it is more closely paid attention to than a banner ad and you do not run the risk of someone accidentally clicking onto it.

There are literally millions of websites on the Internet. Web advertisers are familiar with the traffic that these sites generate. Your fee will be based upon the amount of traffic the website expects to see.

In addition, the length of your video matters a great deal in video advertising. It is best to keep it short. Not only is it cheaper to run the video ad this way, but people generally have a short attention span and something that is too long generally bores them.

Take a look at television commercials prior to embarking on your video ad venture. See which ones you pay attention to and which ones you can't even remember. See which ones you get bored of and dread every time they come on. Your video advertising is similar to this. No one wants to constantly see a long, boring video all over the Internet. A short, entertaining video that is used sporadically, however, will generate more interest and may even develop a cult following.

People are crazy about Internet videos. They use them on their personal Internet community pages such as Twitter and Facebook and often e-mail them to their friends and relatives. This can happen to you. You may come up with an advertisement that is clever, entertaining and brings you instant Internet notoriety.

If you decide not to use a professional agency, you will be able to put the video anywhere that is free. You can also act as your own advertising agent and make deals with certain websites yourself. This can be difficult and you should have some knowledge about copyright laws and legal contracts before doing this. And unlike the professionals, you may not know much about the website. Unfortunately, on the Internet, websites come and go. You would hate to make a deal and pay money to advertise on a site that closes within the next week.

If you use a professional Internet advertising agency, chances are that you will hit your target audience with your video ad and will find it more successful than a banner ad. Your video will be able to go just about any place on the Internet that your banner ad can go, or your word ad. The difference will be that more people will pay attention to what you are trying to sell.

How Do I Begin?

Now that you have learned the many benefits of advertising using videos on the Internet to generate more business, you are probably asking yourself how to begin using this new media. This depends upon whether you want to self market your video on your website or if you want to use an Internet advertising agency to self market for you.

The one way a business knows if its advertising is succeeding on the Internet is through statistics. If, for example, you are advertising on Google, you will be notified of the amount of times a person clicked onto your ad each month and will have to pay accordingly. Google will then share some of that revenue with those websites that allowed them to place the ad on their site. This is the way that Internet advertising works.

It is important for you to know how many people click on your ads for many reasons. First of all, if you are advertising on several different sites, and the stats for one site are much higher than the others, you may want to consider changing advertising strategies. If Google is using your ad on a blog and it is getting no activity, this may mean that you owe them no extra money, but it also means that no one is interested in your ad on that website. By keeping track of your statistics regarding ad views, you can ascertain which sites are worth more advertising and which sites are not.

If you are planning on self promoting your own video on your website, you most likely have a stat counter that tells you how often people visit your site. After you have added your video, see if there is a difference. Chances are, there will be. There are also software programs that allow you to find out how often your video is viewed on your site. If you see that it is being viewed over and over, but your site stats do not reflect the number of video viewings, chances are that you have a clever ad. You may want to market it elsewhere. If you see that very few people are bothering to view your video advertisement on your website, you may want to try a different video that will attract more attention. This is one way you can ascertain how good your business video is.

If you decide to promote your video on a free space such as You Tube, you will be given statistics. Each video shows the public how many times it has been viewed and they are even rated. People may even make comments on them. If you come up with something truly unique, you may find that your video gets featured as "most popular" and gets something like 10,000 views a day. This does not necessarily mean that you will get 10,000 new patients, but chances are that you will get a few new people at your website.

So where you begin is up to how much money you want to spend, if any, and how much advertising you want to do. If you have a large practice and have a substantial budget for advertising, you may want to begin by hiring an agency that specializes in video ads to come up with something clever for your video campaign. If you hire someone to make a video for you, you can purchase the rights to the video so that it cannot be used elsewhere without your permission. Some companies will want to retain the rights. This is something that should and can be negotiated with whatever company you decide to hire to create your video.

If music is played in your video that is not within the public domain, you may have to pay for a license to use the music. This is called a synchronization license and can be obtained from the publisher. The publisher will charge by the amount of seconds the song is used in the ad as well as how often the ad is used. This means that in addition to paying your Internet advertiser each time someone views your video, you will also have to pay the publisher. The amount of such a license generally depends upon the popularity of the song. You can either try to negotiate this yourself or have an attorney knowledgeable in copyright and licensing laws to negotiate the fee for you.

Once the video is completed to your satisfaction, you will present it to your Internet advertiser who will advise you on where it should be featured and how often. If you are currently using an Internet advertiser such as Google, and are finding some success with banner ads, you may want to continue with the same websites. You will want to find out the difference in how many people view your video ad as compared to your banner ad to see how effective this advertising is.

There are different types of video ads. Some pop up and just start playing the minute you hit on the ad, and others have a "play" button. You may want to set up the option to have the potential customer play the video instead of it just playing to see if they are truly interested in the video and the ad.

You will still have to have some sort of written advertisement so that people know what your video is. You can have a video still and something that says "If you want to learn more about how to get designer shoes at the best prices on the Internet, click here." At that point, the video will play. The good thing about video advertising as opposed to print advertising on the Internet is that the customer will most likely not hit the ad by accident.

Many websites, in order to gain profit from ads that they receive from Google and other sources, use little tricks to get people to hit on the ads. This is not what you want. You are paying for the advertising so that you can continue to develop your business and increase your profit, not support various websites. Make sure that the websites that you are advertising on are not doing this. Such tricks include moving objects that get close to where the customer is trying to click to see information. They click, go into the ad and get annoyed. This does nothing for your business.

If you want to start just by putting a video on your company website, just do it! You can either have an ad agency that specializes in this to create a video for you, or you can make your own video. Again, this depends upon your advertising budget. But there are many companies out there that are hungry for this sort of work and you may be surprised that the cost is not as high as you may think.

Depending upon your website, you may want to make a home made video. Sometimes these can be more entertaining than the slick, professional videos and people generally like to watch them. Consider the popularity of YouTube, which features many home made videos as well as the old program "America's Best Home Made Videos." There can be something more refreshing in a home made video and may actually generate more trust within your customer.

www.ifusedentalmarketing.com

Still, another way is to use a clip from a film. You may not want to go as far as the "Psycho" clip that the shower filter company used, but there are thousands of films in the public domain that are available. If you can find something appropriate that advertises your company, why not use it?

Come up with a plan on how much you want to spend, whether or not you want a professional to make the video or you want to make it yourself and where you want the video to be placed on the Internet. This all depends on budget. But even those companies with a low advertising budget will benefit tremendously from advertising by video on the Internet. It is just simply more entertaining

What About Video Content?

Now that you are ready to begin using video advertising on the Internet, you are probably wondering what type of content you should put in your video? How long should it be? Should it be funny? Should it feature people or just items?

The one thing that you want to make sure that you express in your video is your practice. This seems like common sense, but advertising executives in the 1980s often came out with "clever" ads that did not exactly represent what their client was selling. These ads were mostly for upscale products that were supposed to appeal to "intellectuals" and not to the commoners. The ads were mostly pretentious and not successful.

While you do not want to be obtuse about your practice, you also do not want to keep hammering the name throughout the ad as if the client is either demented or deaf. Keywords work well with SEO articles, but are not necessary in a video ad. You want to make sure that you mention the name of the practice at least twice, the benefits of going to the practice and where you are located. You can do this quickly, but must make sure that the name of your business and website is clear.

If you hire someone to create your video, they will most likely present you with several ideas. Advertising people are experts in marketing and very creative. They may come up with the perfect ad. But it is going to cost you. They will, however, be able to come up with the right way to present the product and your business with the right amount of information, without overdoing it. You can choose one of their ideas if it is something that suits you.

Suppose, however, you want to make your own video ad? This is relatively easy to do as camcorders are easily accessible and relatively inexpensive. With some imagination, you may be able to come up with something creative that will be remembered.

Sometimes, the best known commercials on television are those that featured interesting characters that were difficult to forget. Those of us in Chicago know the "Empire Carpet Man" and would probably recognize him more easily than we would the Vice President. The Empire Carpet company began filming their commercials in the early 1970s using an actor. People assumed he was the owner of Empire Carpets, and he became so popular that they have continued to use the actor since. This was a low budget commercial, but it made the carpet company a household name in Chicago.

There have been others who have stood out as well. "Crazy Larry" in New York. He owned an electronics store and used to shout and scream like a crazy man. The commercial was very well known, not only in New York City, but across the country. And it did wonders for his store. This was another low budget ad and no actors were needed as Crazy Larry himself did his own advertising.

There have been others who have done this with much success. In just about every city, there is a commercial character that people remember. Even today, most of us know the Bob Evans' "Sun" man. These characters stick in our mind because of one thing - they are people.

People relate to other people. Particularly those who stand out. This does not mean you have to act like a lunatic or dress like the sun to perform in your own video. But if you have a pleasant appearance, a good voice, can appear before a camera without being nervous, you may have what it takes to perform in your own Internet video ad.

If you add a bit of humor to your ad, you can generally get more attention and publicity. Remember that you want to make sure that your ad is entertaining. This is the key and the entire purpose of video advertising on the Internet. Just as a film producer wants their film to be entertaining, so does an advertiser. And if you are creating your own ad, you have to make sure that your ad not only gives the viewer pertinent information about your practice, but also entertains.

Which type of advertisement on television sticks out in your mind? Chances are, it is either those you remember from your youth, those with interesting characters, or those interesting commercials shown during the Super Bowl.

Some of these advertisements cost quite a bit of money to film and even more to broadcast during the Super Bowl. Others cost very little to film and were only on local channels but generated just as much publicity.

Many of the most successful commercials and advertisements contained quite a bit of humor. Americans love humor and funny videos are often passed around the Internet through e-mail. Most people get several of these types of funny videos from their friends and relatives in their e-mail each week. Again, Americans love to be entertained.

So if you decide to act in your own video Internet ad, be sure to do so with a sense of humor. No one will want to watch someone drone on in a monotone voice about how great his website that sells discounted DVDs is. They will be bored quickly and press stop. If you have an outgoing personality and pleasant speaking voice, you may be able to manage your own video ad.

A video ad featuring a person is more effective than one that just features an object. Even if you have a real estate brokerage website and want to feature virtual tours of homes, be sure to put a little human quality in with the video. Humanize your video for your audience.

You do not have to be Cecil B. DeMille to come up with a good video for your website or as a way to generate business over the Internet. You simply have to have a bit of an imagination and a way to come across as honest and a person with whom someone would want to do business.

As much as you want your video to stand out, you also do not want to make a video that is so entertaining that it detracts from your purpose. Remember that the purpose of video advertising on the Internet is to draw more patients and business. You want to use this as a way to add to the revenue from your business, not to become an Internet star.

No matter whether you have a professional create your Internet video or if you decide to do this to it yourself, you want to make sure that your audience knows the name of your practice, what you are selling and how they can contact you so that you make a sale.

You can also use your video, if you decide to create it yourself, as a marketing tool to advertise specials and sales by e-mailing the videos to your regular patients. It will seem more personal than a standard e-mail and is also another effective marketing tool and yet another bit of content you can add to your Internet video ad.

How Effective Is Internet Video Advertising? Ask Dr. Henry.

So just how effective is using video advertising on the Internet to generate more income for your business? Ask Dr. Henry.

Dr. Henry purchased a practice in Massachusetts a few years ago. It was a charming old Victorian home that needed quite a bit of work. He invested most of his savings into fixing it up and getting it ready for what he was sure to be a bevy of patients. Unfortunately, after a few months, Dr. Henry found he was not getting the patients that he needed to make a profit, let alone do the continued repairs on the old home.

A friend who was computer savvy, helped Dr. Henry by creating a website for him. The website was done in a professional manner and featured photos of all of the rooms in the lovely old home. His friend showed Dr. Henry how to try to promote his website on the Internet. He invested more money into making sure that his practice was listed in certain websites that featured practices. This did manage to generate a bit of business for Dr. Henry. He found that he was getting more business by way of the Internet than he was through the many other companies with whom he did business. And definitely much more business than the print ads that seemed to cost a fortune.

Business was getting better, but it still wasn't as good as Dr. Henry had hoped. Although he wasn't a greedy man and not out to make a fortune, he wanted to earn a decent profit. Dr. Henry was a widower and he had invested most of his savings in this business. He had always wanted to run his own practice. He had a pleasing personality and the patients liked him. In addition, Dr. Henry liked the idea of having people in the building. He was lonely since the death of his wife.

Dr. Henry began using the computer a bit more often as well. His friend instructed him on how to navigate the Internet and with his friend's help, Dr. Henry began expanding his web page. He included letters from pleased patients and a message board.

Another friend who was even more savvy with the computer was familiar with the new trend in video advertising on the Internet. She thought that she could do wonders with Dr. Henry's website and make it even more interesting. While Dr. Henry's website certainly was professional and pleasant, it feature only photos of the building and the rooms. There was no photo of Dr. Henry on the site.

Dr. Henry's friend, Joan, was inventive and had a camcorder. She often filmed videos for different websites where she was paid for tutorials. She was also an active participant on You Tube. She thought it might be fun to film a video ad for Dr. Henry's practice. It could easily be added to the website and may even bring in more business.

When Joan approached Dr. Henry with the idea, he was a little reluctant. He didn't want to be shown in front of the camera. He was an elderly, kind looking man with a nice grin, but didn't feel like "movie star material" as he put it. Joan explained to him that it was better to be an average person with a pleasant demeanor and honest face in advertising.

Dr. Henry was a bit apprehensive, because he would have to appear in the video, but Joan assured him that he would be a natural.

Joan was good with editing and filming. She began the advertisement with a very short clip of Dr. Henry's practice on the video. The over voice, which was Joan's said "You can settle for less in a practice, or you can visit the best practice in MA. She then featured Dr. Henry, who was more comfortable seated than standing. He was pictured in front of a warm fireplace and several patients were sitting in the main lobby area

The video then featured some of the patient rooms and the lobby area. It ended with a video shot of the outside of the practice looking at the front door.

Dr. Henry was thrilled with the video. Never a technical whiz, he was surprised to see how easy it was for Joan to complete such an advertisement. And she did it all on her computer. Then she uploaded it to his website.

The results were immediate. People loved the advertisement. Dr. Henry began to receive a lot of calls from people who wanted to visit his practice. The video advertisement, although simple and not very costly, had certainly done wonders for his business.

But that wasn't all. Joan wasn't finished with trying to help her friend Dr. Henry. She put the video on You Tube. It began to get a lot of views and soon became very popular. People started commenting on the humor and copying the video to send to their friends by e-mail. Some people even portrayed the entertaining video on their blogs.

Soon Dr. Henry's phone was ringing off the hook. He had more business than he could handle. He had money to fix up two more rooms in the attic that he had neglected and was able to take in more patients. Before long, Dr. Henry had one of the most popular practices in Massachusetts.

Dr. Henry was always a good practice owner. His practice was always clean, he was kind to his patients and the establishment was lovely. But because people didn't know about it, he wasn't getting the patients he could have.

Because of the Internet website and video advertising, Dr. Henry's business, that was once just getting by, was now bustling. Bookings had to be made months in advance. The video still circulated for a while on the Internet. And because Dr. Henry was such a good host and ran such a good practice, he had many patients who came back over and over again.

This is just one example of how a little bit of Internet know-how, a video camera, a bit of the knowledge of what you can use on the Internet in your ads and a little imagination saved a business. It began with the website and ended with a very successful ad campaign. And it saved a retiree's business.

Do you still wonder how effective Internet video advertising can be? Dr. Henry's story is just one of many. Many businesses are discovering the importance of advertising on a media that 82 percent of Americans use. Many of them are realizing that entertaining people with clever video ads are more effective than word ads. Video advertising on the Internet is the way of the future.

Dr. Henry's story is not unique. It is a true success story and amazing because it was done by an amateur. But there are thousands of businesses who are discovering that video advertising on the Internet is not only drawing more attention to their business, but increasing their sales and adding to their revenue.

www.ifusedentalmarketing.com

What Other Visual Methods Can I Use?

You have now probably decided to implement the use of video technology to not only draw patients to your website, but make your site more appealing and increase your new patient counts. But that is not all that you can do to increase sales from your website.

Remember how we talked about that people are very visual. This means that you want to show not only videos on your website but other photographs and visual products as well. This ranges from clip art, cartoons, photographs and even animation. There are certain software programs that will allow you to create an animated character that can "walk your client through" your website. You want to make sure that this character that is small, does not overpower the website, it pleasant and harmless looking and that the customer has the power to turn the little animated guy off. While this may appeal to some people, some might find it annoying.

Also, you have to remember that some people will be perusing your website while at work. They probably will not be supposed to be doing this, but they will be doing it anyway. Many people are getting fired for "Internet abuse." As a matter of fact, it is one of the leading causes of people losing their jobs in the United States. You will want to make sure that both your video and your animated character have a volume or mute control.

Clip art is always fun as are funny cartoons. You will have make certain, however, that the clip art that you use is public and free. There are millions of free clip art products both available over the Internet as well as in software. These are all within the public domain and free to use. Why not use them?

In addition, there are hundreds of photographs and cartoons that lie within the public domain that you can add to your website. If you can find a cartoon that pertains to your business that is a free cartoon, why not use it in your website? You can even get a little creative and edit the cartoon to mention the name of your business.

Still another way to increase sales using visual elements on your website is by the use of coupons that can be printed by the customer and used. People love coupons and many websites are using this marketing method to not only attract new sales, but also to gauge how many people are visiting their website.

If you are not an expert at setting up a website, and few of us are, why not have a professional create a website for you? There are many companies and individuals who do this for businesses. If you have a small budget, you can hire a person who is attending technical college to learn how to set up a website. You will be surprised at the knowledge this young person will have and they will charge you much less than a professional company. You may even get more innovation; you never know. The kid that you hire to create your website might be the next brightest new talent.

Once you have created your website, get some opinions from friends and colleagues on the site itself. Remember that you will want to make the website easy to read, easy to understand, easy to navigate and above all, attractive and entertaining. This means using any visual means that you have at your disposal, including video, you will have a website that will appear professional and you will be using all modern means to attract patients, generate new leads and increase sales and profits.

Some Video Marketing Tips

By now you realize just how much videos added to your website can do to not only improve your website, but generate leads and sales. The type of video that you use will have to depend on the type of practice you have. You can use video in many different ways. The examples given of Dr. Henry's practice and the shower filter company both used humor in a positive way to attract patients.

There are other ways that you can use video as well, without having to pay any fees to producers who may own the video. Remember in the last chapter how we talked about coupons? People like to save money. They like to feel that they are getting a deal.

Observe commercials on television. They will often say that if you call within a certain amount of minutes, you will get an extra product or discount. You can do this as well. Either on your own website, through e-mail or even on a free video site, such as You Tube.

For example, suppose you have an excess of a certain product you would really like to move. One way to do it is to introduce the product in your own home made video. Tell people how wonderful this product is, and that it is now available at a special rate. And if they call or order right away, they can get free shipping. Make sure that this is cost effective to you. If you have your own business, you probably already know about different ways to market certain products. One method includes marking the product up a bit to cover the "free shipping." You do not want to lose money on this promotion. However, this will only work if it is a new product that you have not previously advertised on your website. If you have this product on the website for $24.99 and suddenly you are sending out a video that it is now "marked down" to $29.99 including free shipping, your patients will feel cheated and you will lose your credibility. This method only works with overstock that you cannot move or a brand new product that has not yet been advertised.

So you make your video and put it on your website. Is that good enough? No. You want to make sure that you send your video to all of your patients through e-mail, particularly those who have purchased the product in the past. E-mail is free advertising, it doesn't get any better than that.

You can also advertise your product on You Tube or other free avenues.

This is not going to cost you a dime and may generate much income, as well as rid you of some products that you are dying to get rid of.

No matter what type of practice you own, use marketing techniques combined with video in your sales. Sure, the videos on your website can be entertaining and make your site more attractive. These alone will generate more sales. But when you combine them with old-fashioned marketing techniques, you've really got is a winner.

Move Into The Future

By now you should know all about how video advertising on the Internet can draw more people to your website, give you new leads on patients, and increase your sales and revenue. By now you know that people are visual and like to be entertained. You have been given a number of examples on how you can use video in your website and Internet advertising to your advantage.

You know the difference between hiring an advertising firm to create your video. You know that you can easily create your own video and easily add it to your website. You know the difference between advertising via video on other websites, which will cost you money, as well as implementing this technology on your own website.

Advertising has always been with us. Prior to television, advertising was seen in print. In the newspapers, magazines and on billboards. Prior to that, they had metal signs to let people know about their product. Anyone who is in business knows that in order to sell something, you have a better chance of making a sale if people actually know about your business and what exactly it is that you are selling.

After print ads came radio ads. Then people began watching television and it became necessary for commercials to be filmed. Early commercials on television were often very crude, but somehow, people still remember these old ads. It became apparent to companies that in order to keep up with the competition, they had to have a good advertising campaign. They hired the best advertising executives that they could find to come up with slogans, gimmicks, print ads, jingles and commercials. Many of us still remember the commercial jingles from the past, which do not seem to be used that much anymore. Television ads have, like television, become more sophisticated.

The Internet has also become more sophisticated. You now know that most people in the United States use the Internet. Some people use the Internet a little too much. Internet addiction is beginning to become a problem. People use the Internet all the time, even at work when they are supposed to be doing their jobs. For most of us in the United States, the first thing we do when we get up in the morning is check our e-mail.

Camcorders, once an item people used to film their children, have come down significantly in price since the late 1980s. They are small, easy to use and the videos are very easy to upload onto the Internet. So easy, as a matter of fact, that people are using videos for just about everything. Writing sites that used to feature only text media, now offer creative types to submit videos as tutorials for money. They realize that many people learn better by seeing how something is done rather than just reading about it.

Just about anywhere you can ad text on the Internet, you can ad video. Most online communities allow videos on their website. They cost nothing. Dating sites are using videos as a form of "matching" people.

There is much competition between online dating sites, and many are realizing that those that feature videos instead of blurry photographs are becoming more popular and getting more members.

Websites for businesses have evolved from simple sites that offered an array of products to those that feature flash videos, music and entertainment as you shop. Banner ads that people click on accidentally that end up costing companies money are soon to be obsolete. There is a new technology, a better technology, to advertise your business. Video. And it is just as easy to use and more effective.

The way you use video on your website is limited only by your imagination. You can use it to depict a peaceful scene that is pleasant to view and soothing to sell your aromatherapy products, or you can use it to depict scenes from a travel spot that are just breathtaking.

You can also implement humor to make people want to stay on your website. You can change the video periodically to keep them coming back. You can do anything you want.

By now you have realized that sending an e-mail that says you have a sale on shirts is not as effective as sending a video e-mail that really grabs the recipient's attention and makes them look. You know that when you combine this form of media advertising with marketing tools, you can mix the old with the new and generate a lot more sales on your website.

You know that there are many different free outlets that will enable you to upload your video for free. While you should not depend solely on a website like YouTube to promote your business, particularly because you cannot really target your audience, you can promote the name of your business and if your video is funny and clever enough, this free form of advertising may draw people to your website.

Video advertising on the Internet is not very new, but is still at the beginning stages. It has proven to be very popular and effective.

www.ifusedentalmarketing.com

Internet advertisers are reporting that video ads are much more effective than print ads and many are trying to get their clients to switch to this media.

More companies are coming up with different ways to continue to improve video technology on the web, including Microsoft. They realize that video advertising, particularly on websites, is now imminent. More websites are now beginning to add videos to attract patients and boost sales. Those who will cling on to the past will soon be left in the past. Just as the businesses once were that refused to advertise on television.

Now that you know all there is to know about the different ways you can use video advertising on your website to generate leads and sales, you should be eager to begin. Whether you hire an outside company or film your own video is up to you. Either way, now is the time to pull yourself into the future of this brilliant technology.

Conclusion

We're thrilled that you have chosen to take advantage of our guide, and we wish you amazing success.

Thanks so much for the time you have dedicated to learning how to get the most advantages from Local Marketing. Local Marketing has come to stay in the market forever.

To Your Success,

Chris Pistorius
iFuse Dental Marketing
www.ifusedentalmarketing.com

www.ingramcontent.com/pod-product-compliance
Lightning Source LLC
Chambersburg PA
CBHW051718170526
45167CB00002B/709